Empowered by Economics

Empowered by Economics

Macro Economics

Sonia Gupta

GenNext Publication

First Published, 2020

Published by

GenNext Publication
5, Ansari Road
Daryaganj, New Delhi-110002
Phone: 9811692060
E-mail: gennextpublication@hotmail.com

Printed at: G. Print Process, Delhi.

Cataloging in Publication Data—DK
Courtesy: D.K. Agencies (P) Ltd. <docinfo@dkagencies.com>

Gupta, Sonia, author.
Empowered by economics : macroeconomics for class-XII / by Mrs. Sonia Gupta.
pages cm
ISBN 9789353242145

1. Macroeconomics—Examinations, questions, etc. I. Title.

LCC HB172.5.G87 2020 | DDC 339 23

Contents

Foreword

"Empowered by Econornics" a book on Macro Economics authored by Ms. Sonia Gupta has thoroughly impressed me, first the writer has made intensive study of the curriculum prescribed by CBSE for class XII Economics and secondly, she has gone into depth of the marking scheme, weightage of marks and project work as prescribed by CBSE.

The author has done lot of research on various kinds of questions generally expected in Board's Examination. She has framed the questions unit wise and given answers to each question in simple language and point wise. I will recommend that the class XII students, who are preparing for the Board's examination will find the book very useful attempting the Macro Economics part in the examination paper, I also feel the students will have good understanding of the concepts and learn the correct approach in answering the questions.

S.K. Bhattacharya
Former Principal
Bal Bharati Public School
Sir Ganga Ram Hospital Marg.

A-129, Ashok Vihar, Phase-III, Delhi-110052.
Phone : (Mob.) 9811240804 (Resi.) 011-27304044, 27306638
(Off.) 27028600, 27028700 (Extn.) 35, 27017900 (Direct)
Email: bbpstc@gmail.com

Advisor
Child Education Society

Chairman
Nursery Teacher Training Institute

Secretary/Manager
Bal Bharati Public School
Pushpanjali Enclave,
Pitampura, Delhi

Chairman
BBPS Training Centre
Pushpanjali Enclave,
Pitampura, Delhi

Chairman
Bal Bharati Nursery School
Maulana Azad, Delhi and
Sec. 25, Rohini, Delhi

Preface

This book is a culmination of different student experiences which has helped me in writing this book. Identification of a student's problem was my first task which led me to create a book which not only encompasses all the student's needs but also help them understand Economics in an easier manner. Empowered by Economics is the result of my 16 years of teaching experience. Every interaction with students, teachers and other professors has helped me to write this piece.

This book has been written in Question – Answers form, which will not only help the students to understand the concept easily but will also help them memorize the content easily. This book will help them crack the toughest of exams with ease, because of its Student-Centric approach.

Suggestions from students and teachers would be highly appreciated.

Sonia Gupta

Email: sonia.7618@gmail.com

Ph: +91-9911555234

Part - A
Introductory Macroeconomics

Unit 1: National Income and Related Aggregates (28 Periods)

- What is Macroeconomics?
- Basic concepts in macroeconomics: consumption goods, capital goods, final goods, intermediate goods; stocks and flows; gross investment and depreciation.
- Circular flow of income (two-sector model);
- Methods of calculating National Income – Value Added or Product method, Expenditure method, Income method.
- Aggregates related to National Income: Gross National Product (GNP), Net National Product (NNP), Gross and Net Domestic Product (GDP and NDP) – at market price, at factor cost; Real and Nominal GDP. GDP and Welfare

Unit 2: Money and Banking (15 Periods)

- Money – meaning and supply of money – Currency held by the public and net demand deposits held by commercial banks.
- Money creation by the commercial banking system.
- Central bank and its functions (example of the Reserve Bank of India): Bank of issue, Govt. Bank, Banker's Bank, Control of Credit through Bank Rate, CRR, SLR, Repo Rate and Reverse Repo Rate, Open Market Operations, Margin requirement.

Unit 3: Determination of Income and Employment (27 Periods)

- Aggregate demand and its components.
- Propensity to consume and propensity to save (average and marginal).
- Short-run equilibrium output; investment multiplier and its mechanism.
- Meaning of full employment and involuntary unemployment.
- Problems of excess demand and deficient demand; measures to correct them changes in government spending, taxes and money supply.

Unit 4: Government Budget and the Economy (15 Periods)

- Government budget – meaning, objectives and components.
- Classification of receipts – revenue receipts and capital receipts;
- Classification of expenditure – revenue expenditure and capital expenditure.
- Measures of government deficit – revenue deficit, fiscal deficit, primary deficit their meaning.

Unit 5: Balance of Payments (15 Periods)

- Balance of payments account – meaning and components; balance of payments deficit meaning.
- Foreign exchange rate – meaning of fixed and flexible rates and managed floating. Determination of exchange rate in a free market.

Unit – I

National Income and Related Aggregates

1.1 Basic concepts of National Income

(i) Concept of consumption and capital goods.

(ii) Concept of Intermediate and final goods.

(iii) Concept of stock and flow.

(iv) Concept of current and capital transfer.

(v) Concept of factor income and transfer income.

(vi) Economic territory.

(vii) Resident.

(viii) Concept of circular flow of income.

1.2 Aggregates related to National Income

(i) Investment (Gross and Net).

(ii) Depreciation and its causes.

(iii) Capital loss.

(iv) Concept of net factor income from abroad.

(v) Concept of Net Indirect Tax (NIT).

(vi) Definitions of basic aggregates.

(vii) Basic formulae.

1.3 Measurement of National Income

(i) Concept of value-added method, Income Method, Expenditure Method.

(ii) Steps and precautions of all the three methods.

(iii) Reconciliation of all the three methods.

(iv) Transactions.

1.4 GDP Welfare

(i) Meaning of welfare.

(ii) Real GDP and Nominal GDP.

(iii) Real Income and Nominal Income.

(iv) Limitations of per capital Real GDP as an indicator of Economic Welfare.

1.1 BASIC CONCEPTS OF NATIONAL INCOME

One Mark Question

Q. 1 What are consumption goods?

Ans.: Goods which are capable of satisfying the wants of the consumer directly are called consumption goods.

For Example: Clothes, furniture, Vehicles etc.

Q. 2 What are capital goods?

Ans.: Goods which are capable of being used for producing other goods are called capital goods.

For Example: Building, Equipments, Machines etc.

Q. 3 What are intermediate goods or intermediate product?

Ans.: Goods which are used for:

(i) further production.

(ii) resold or completely used up during the same year are called intermediate goods.

For Example: Milk purchased by a restaurant as it is used for resale.

Q. 4 What are final goods or final product?

Ans.: Goods which are used for consumption and investment purpose are called final goods.

For Example: Milk purchased by a household for consumption purpose.

Q. 5. Define Stock.

Ans.: Those variables whose magnitude is measured at a particular point of time is called stock.

For Example: Capital, Wealth, Inventory etc.

Q. 6. Define Flow.

Ans.: Those variables whose magnitude is measured over a period of time.

For Example: Savings, Losses etc.

Q. 7 Define Economic Territory.

Ans.: It refers to the geographical area administered by the government having free movement of goods, persons and capital.

Q. 8 Define Resident.

Ans.: A resident is an individual or an institution whose centre of economic interest lies in the economic territory of that country in which he lives or is located.

Q. 9 What is a transfer?

Ans.: A transfer is a one-way transaction of providing a good, service or an asset without receiving anything in return.

Q. 10 Define current transfer.

Ans.: Current transfer are those transfers which are made out of current income of the payer.

For Example: Scholarship, Gifts, Pension etc.

Q. 11 Define capital transfer.

Ans.: Capital transfers are those transfers which are made out of wealth or capital of the payer.

For Example:lump sum payment to households affected by natural calamities. (like Flood, Earthquake).

Q. 12 Define factor income.

Ans.: It is defined as income received by factors of production for rendering factor services in the production process.

For Example: Rent, Interest, Profit etc.

Q. 13 Define transfer income.

Ans.: It is defined as income received without rendering any productive service in return.

For Example: Scholarship, Gifts, Pension etc.

Q. 14 Define circular flow of income.

Ans.: It refers to the cycle of income generation in the production phase which is distributed as factor payments to the households, and spent by the households as final expenditure on the purchase of goods and services produced by the production units.

Q. 15 State the three phases of circular flow of income.

Ans.: The three phases are: –

(i) Production Phase (Income is generated in this phase).

(ii) Income Distribution Phase (Income is distributed to households).

(iii) Expenditure Phase (Consumption households expenditure flows from household to firms).

Q. 16 Define Real Flow.

Ans.: It is the flow of goods and services between firms and households.

Q. 17 Define Money Flow.

Ans.: It is the flow of money between firms and households.

3-4 Marks short Questions

Q. 1 Define Consumption Goods. How it is different from Capital Goods.

OR

Differentiate between Consumption and Capital Goods.

Ans.:	**Consumption Goods**	**Capital Goods**
	Meaning: Goods which are capable of satisfying the wants of the consumers directly are called consumption goods.	***Meaning:*** Goods which are capable of being used for producing other goods are called Capital Goods.
	Generation of Income: These goods are not used for generating income. *Example:* Car, TV etc.	***Generation of Income:*** These goods are used for generating income. *Example:* Building, Machines etc.

Q. 2 Give the classification of consumption Goods.

Ans.: Consumption goods are classified into following categories:–

1. **Durable Consumer Goods:** Goods which are used again and again.

   For Example: Car, TV, Refrigerator etc.

2. **Non-Durable Consumer Goods:** Goods which cannot be used more than once i.e. used up in a single act of consumption.

   For Example: Food items etc

Q. 3 Give the classification of capital goods.

Ans.: Capital goods are classified into following categories:

1. **Durable Consumer Goods:** Goods which provide services for a long time to the production units.

   For Example: Building, Machinery etc.

2. **Non-Durable Consumer Goods:** Goods which are single use capital goods.

For Example: Stocks of raw material etc.

Note: CLASSIFICATION OF THESE TWO GOODS DEPEND UPON THEIR USE.

For Example:

- A car purchased by a family – Consumption Goods.
- A car purchased by a factory – Capital Goods.

Q. 4 Distinguish between Intermediate Products and Final Products.

Ans.:	Intermediate Products	Final Products.
	Meaning: Goods which are used for i) further production. ii) resold or completely used up during the same year are called intermediate goods.	***Meaning:*** Goods used for consumption and investment purposes are called final goods.
	Calculation in National Income: These goods are not included in calculation of national income.	***Calculation in National Income:*** These goods are included in calculation of national income.
	Demand: These goods have derived demand. *For Example:* Milk purchased by a restaurant for further production.	***Demand:*** These goods have a direct demand. *For Example:* Milk purchased by a household for consumption purposes.

Q. 5 "No product is always final or always intermediate" Explain.

Ans.: No goods or service is either always intermediate or always final. It may be intermediate for one purchaser and final for another purchaser.

It depends upon the nature of its use.

For Example:

- Bread purchased by a shop is an intermediate good.
- Bread purchased by a consumer for consumption is a final good.

Q. 6 What are the exceptions in case of defence services?

Ans.: Some durable capital goods are treated as intermediate goods in defence services as they are treated as raw materials for producing defence services. These include:

(i) Weapons used for destruction like bombs, rockets, missiles etc.

(ii) Equipments used to deliver these weapons such as trucks, vehicles, launchers etc.

Q. 7 Distinguish between Stock and Flow.

Ans.:	**Stock**	**Flow**
	Meaning: Stock relates to a point of time.	***Meaning:*** Flow relates to a period of time.
	Nature: It is a static concept.	***Nature:*** It is a dynamic concept.
	Time Dimension: It does not have a time dimension. *For Example:* Capital, Inventory, Wealth etc.	***Time Dimension:*** It has a time dimension. *For Example:* Savings, Losses etc.

Q. 8 Distinguish between Current Transfer and Capital Transfer.

Ans.:	**Current Transfer**	**Capital Transfer**
	Meaning: These transfers are made out of current income of the payer.	***Meaning:*** These transfers are made out of wealth or capital of the payer.
	Nature: These are regular transfers.	***Nature:*** These are irregular transfers.
	Examples: • Transfers within the country e.g. scholarships, gifts, pension. • Transfers between the countries e.g. donations, transfer of money by relatives residing abroad.	***Examples:*** • Transfers within the country e.g. capital grants, lump sum payment to households affected by natural calamities. • Transfers between the country e.g. international grants, war damages etc.

Q. 9 Distinguish between Factor Income and Transfer Income.

Factor Income	**Transfer Income**
Meaning: It refers to income received by factors of production for rendering factor services in the production process. ***Concept*** It is an earning concept.	***Meaning:*** It refers to income received without providing any productive services in return. ***Concept*** It is a receipt concept.
Calculation of National Income: These incomes are included in national income. *For Example:* Rent, Interest, Profit, Wages etc.	***Calculation of National Income:*** These incomes are not included in national income. *For Example:* Gifts, pension, Scholarships etc.

Q.10 Explain the Circular Flow of Income.

Ans.: It refers to the cycle of income generation in the production phase which is distributed as factor payments to the households and spent by the households as final expenditure on the purchase of goods and services produced by the production units.

There are only two sectors in the economy Households and Firms.

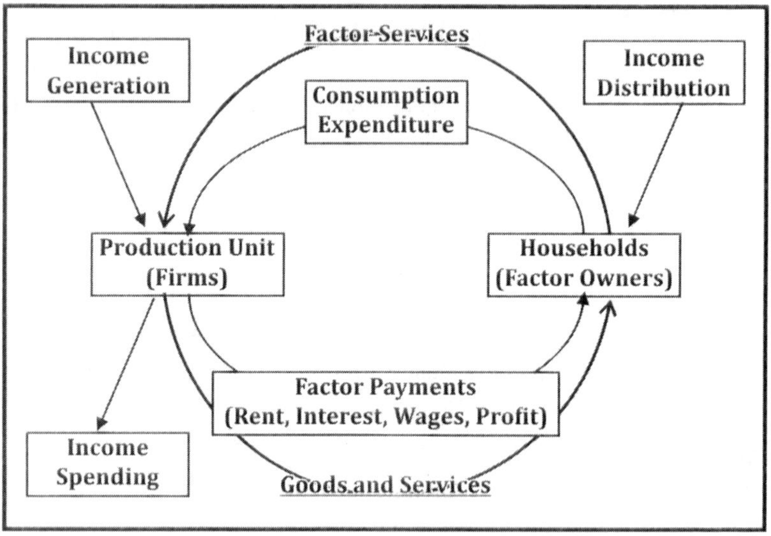

- Households provide factor services to the firms as they are the owners of factors of production.
- Firms provide factor payments in exchange of their factor services.
- So, factor payments flow from firms to households.
- Households purchase goods and services from firms (production units).
- Households make payments to the firms.
- So, consumption expenditure flows from households to the firms.
- This makes the circular flow of income complete.

6 MARKS QUESTIONS

Q.1 Explain the concept of economic or domestic territory.

Ans.: It refers to geographical area administered by a government having free movement of goods, persons and capital. It includes:

1. Ships and aircrafts operated by normal residents between two or more countries.

   For Example: Planes operated by Air India between Dubai and Australia are part of domestic territory of India.

   Planes operated by Dubai airways between India and Australia are part of domestic territory of Dubai.

2. Political frontiers including territorial water and space.

3. Embassies, consulates, military bases etc. of a country located abroad.

   For Example: Indian Embassy in Japan is a part of domestic territory of India.

4. Fishing vessels, natural gas, oil etc. operated by residents in the international waters or other areas where country have exclusive rights of operation.

5. It does not include – Embassies, consultants, military bases etc. of a country.

   For Example: Japanese Embassy in India is a part of domestic territory of Japan.

Q. 2 Explain the concept of normal residents.

Ans.: A resident is an individual or an institution. whose centre of economic interest lies in the economic territory of that country in which he lives or is located.

By centre of economic interest we mean that –

(i) resident lives or is located within economic territory.

(ii) resident carries out the basic economic activities from that location.

* Following Points should be kept in mind:

1. International organizations (like world bank, WHO) are treated as normal residents of international area. They are considered as nonresidents for the country in which they are situated.

2. Employees of international organization are considered residents of the countries to which they belong and not of international area.

   For Example: An American working in international organization located in India will be treated as normal resident of America.

3. Workers from across the border who cross borders regularly to work in the given country are treated as residents of the country where they live and not the residents of the country where they work.

   For Example: Indian workers employed in Nepal on daily wages crossing into Indian territory every week are treated as normal residents of India because they live in India and their economic interest lies in India.

4. Foreign visitors and tourists visiting the particular country for medical treatment, higher studies etc. are not normal residents of that country where they are visiting.

5. Crew members of foreign ships, aircrafts etc. are treated as nonresidents.

BOARD QUESTIONS

Q. 1 **Give two examples of flow concept (2019).**

Q. 2 **Define stock (CBSE 2010).**

Q. 3 **Distinguish between final goods and intermediate goods. Give an example of each (CBSE 2017).**

Q. 4 **Classify into final and intermediate goods, Give reasons. (CBSE 2018).**

(a) Milk purchased by a tea stall.

(b) Bus purchased by a school.

(c) Juice purchased by a student from the school canteen.

Q. 5 **Differentiate between stock and flows (CBSE 2013).**

Q. 6 **Explain the circular flow or income.**

OR

Categories into stock or flow.

(i) Capital

(ii) Saving

(iii) Gross domestic product

(iv) Wealth

(CBSE 2013, 2009)

1. 2 AGGREGATES RELATED TO NATIONAL INCOME

ONE MARK QUESTIONS

Q. 1 Define investment or capital formation.

Ans.: It refers to addition made to the stock of capital during a year. It is also called capital formation.

Q. 2 State the two components of Investment.

Ans.: There are two components of Investment: –

1. Investment in fixed capital (i.e. building, machines etc.). It is called **fixed investment.**
2. Investment in stock of raw material, semi-finished goods etc. It is called **stock investment.**

Q. 3 What is gross investment?

Ans. It refers to total addition of capital goods to the existing capital stock during a given period of time.

Q. 4 What is net investment?

Ans.: It refers to net addition to the capital stock during a given period of time.

OR

It is the net availability of new capital after depreciation of existing capital

Net Investment = Gross Investment – Depreciation.

Q. 5 What is depreciation?

Ans.: It refers to fall in value of fixed capital goods due to normal wear and tear and foreseen obsolescence. It is also known as –

- Current Replacement cost
- Consumption of fixed capital

Q. 6 What are the causes of depreciation?

Ans.: The reasons are:

1. **Normal wear and tear** – It mean fall in the value of fixed asset due to normal use in production.
2. **Foreseen obsolescence** – It means fall in the value due to expected changes in market demand, technology, government policy etc.

Q. 7. What is capital loss?

Ans.: It refers to fall in value of an asset due to unforeseen obsolescence or due to natural calamities like floods, earthquakes etc.

Q. 8 What is NIT (Net Indirect Taxes)?

Ans.: It is the difference between indirect taxes and subsidies

NIT (Net Indirect Taxes) = Indirect Taxes – Subsidies

Q. 9 Define indirect taxes.

Ans.: It refers to those taxes which are imposed by the government on production and sale of goods and services.

For Example: Goods and Service Tax (GST).

Q. 10 Define subsidies.

Ans.: It is a financial assistance given by the government to production units.

Q. 11 What is market price.

Ans.: It is the price paid by the buyer for the final product. It includes the indirect taxes and excludes the subsidies.

Q. 12 What is factor cost.

Ans.: It is the amount paid to factors of production for their contribution in the production process. It is the market price less indirect taxes paid plus subsidies received.

Factor Cost = Market Price – (Indirect Taxes – Subsidies)

= Market Price – Indirect Taxes + Subsidies

Q. 13 What is NFIA (Net Factor Income from Abroad)?

Ans.: It is the difference between factor income received from the rest of the world and factor income paid to the rest of the world.

NFIA = Factor Income earned from abroad – Factor Income paid to abroad.

Q. 14 When NFIA is positive?

Ans.: It is positive when income earned from abroad is more than income paid to abroad.

Q. 15 When NFIA is negative?

Ans.: It is negative when income earned from abroad is less than income paid to abroad.

Q. 16 When NFIA is zero?

Ans.: It is zero when income earned from abroad is equal to income paid to abroad.

Q. 17 What are the components of NFIA?

Ans.: The components of NFIA are: –

1. Net compensation of employees.
2. Net Income from property and entrepreneurship.
3. Net retained earnings.

Q. 18 What are domestic aggregates?

Ans.: Domestic aggregates measure the value of goods and services produced by all units located within domestic territory.

Q. 19 State the domestic concepts.

Ans.: The domestic concepts are: –

1. GDP_{mp} (Gross domestic product at market price).
2. GDP_{fc} (Gross domestic product at factor cost).
3. NDP_{mp} (Net domestic product at market price).
4. NDP_{fc} (Net domestic product at factor cost). It is also called **domestic product.**

Q. 20 What are national aggregates?

Ans.: National aggregates measure the value of goods and services produced by normal residents of a country both inside and outside the economic territory of a country.

Q. 21 State the national concepts.

Ans.: The national concepts are: –

1. GNP_{mp} (Gross national product at market price).
2. GNP_{fc} (Gross national product at factor cost).
3. NNP_{mp} (Net national product at market price).
4. NNP_{fc} or **(National Income)** Net national product at factor cost.

Q. 22 State the formulae to calculate domestic and national aggregates.

Ans.: The following formulae are:–

These three formulae can be shown as –

1.

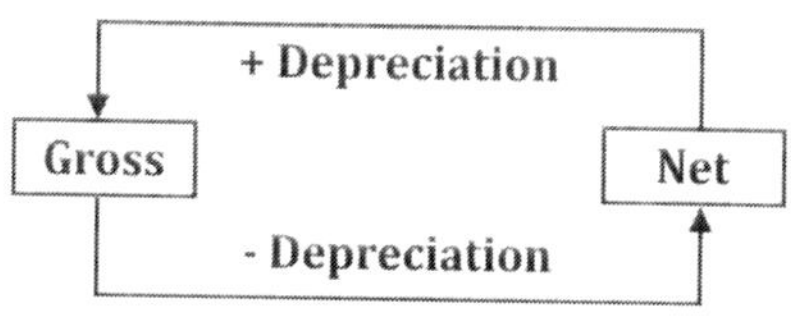

2. 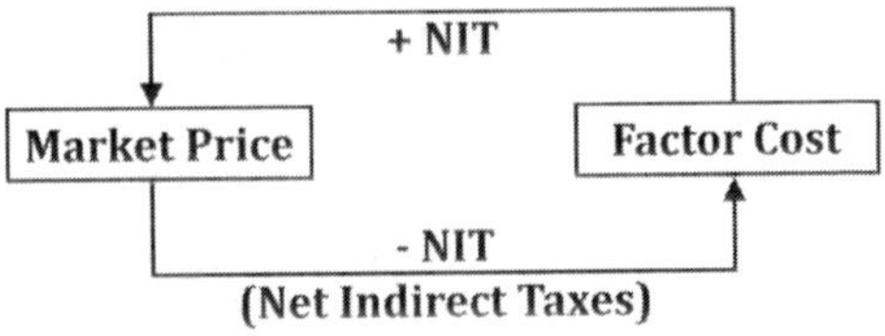

3. 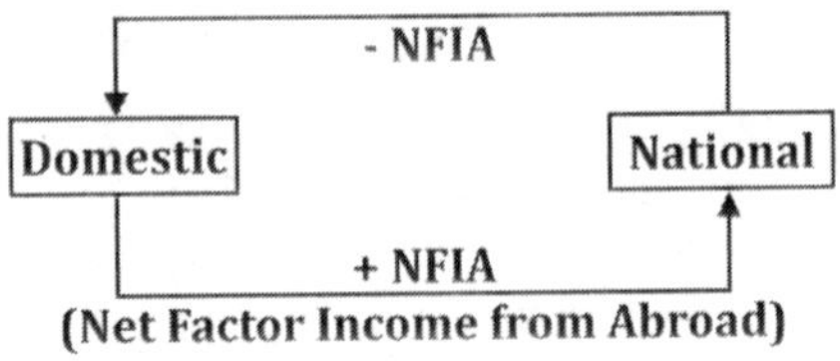

These three formulae can be shown as –

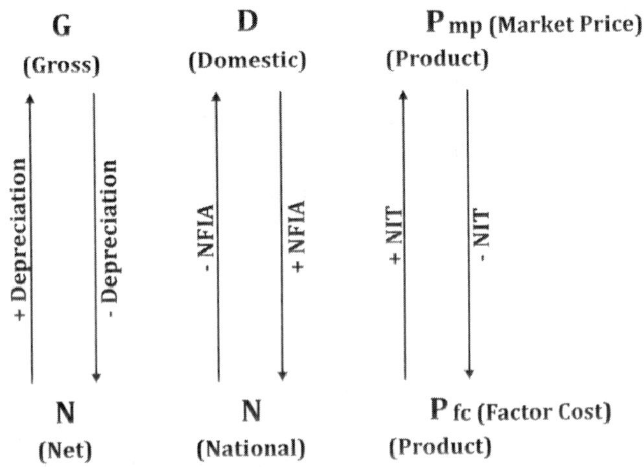

3–4 Marks Questions

Q. 1 Define all the domestic aggregates.

Ans.: The following domestic aggregate may be defined as: –

(a) **GDP_{mp} (Gross domestic product at market price)**. It is the gross market value of final goods and services produced within the domestic territory of a country in a year.

(b) **GDP_{fc} (Gross domestic product at factor cost).** It is gross money value of final goods and services produced within the domestic territory of country in a year.

(c) **NDP_{mp} (Net domestic product at market price).** It is net market value of final goods and services produced within the domestic territory of a country in a year.

(d) **NDP_{fc} (Net domestic product of factor cost).** It is the net money value of final goods and services produced within the domestic territory of a country in a year. It is also called "Domestic Income" or **"Domestic Product".**

Q. 2 How are domestic aggregates related?

Ans.: Domestic aggregates are related as follows: –

(i) $NDP_{mp} = GDP_{mp}$ – depreciation

(ii) $GDP_{fc} = GDP_{mp}$ – indirect taxes + subsidies

(iii) $NDP_{fc} = GDP_{mp}$ – depreciation – NIT

Q. 3 Define all national aggregates.

Ans.: The following national aggregates may be defined as: –

1. **GNP_{mp} (Gross national product at market price).** It is the gross market value of all final goods and services produced in the domestic territory of a country by normal residents during a year including net factor income from abroad.
2. **GNP_{fc} (Gross national product at factor cost).** It is the gross money value of final goods and services produced in the domestic territory of a country by normal residents during a year including net factor income from abroad.
3. **NNP_{mp} (Net national product at market price).** It is the net market value of final goods and services produced within the domestic territory by normal residents during a year including net factor income from abroad.
4. **NNP_{fc} or National Income (Net national product at factor cost).** It is net money value of final goods and service produced within the domestic territory by normal residents during a year including net factor income from abroad. It is also called national product.

Q. 4 How are national aggregate related?

Ans.: National aggregates are related as: –

1. $GNP_{mp} = GDP_{mp} + NFIA$
2. $NNP_{mp} = NDP_{mp} + NFIA$
3. $GNP_{fc} = GDP_{fc} + NFIA$
4. $NNP_{fc} = NDP_{fc} + NFIA$

NUMERICALS ON AGGREGATES OF NATIONAL INCOME

PROBLEM–1:

Calculate NNP_{mp} and GNP_{fc}

	(₹ in Crore)
(i) NDPfc	95
(ii) Net Indirect Taxes	10
(iii) Consumption of fixed capital	15
(iv) NFIA	(–1)

Solution:

NNP_{mp} = NDPfc + NFIA + NIT
= (i) + (iv) + (ii)
= 95 + (–1) + 10
= ₹ 104 Crores

GNP_{fc} = NDPfc + Consumption of fixed capital + NFIA
= (i) + (iii) + (iv)
= 95 + 15 + (–1)
= ₹109 Crores

PROBLEM–2:

Calculate NDPfc and NNPfc

	(₹ in Crore)
(i) GNP_{mp}	300
(ii) NFIA	(–4)
(iii) Depreciation	20
(iv) GST	30
(v) Subsidies	5

Solution:

NDP_{fc} = GNPmp – Depreciation – NFIA – Indirect Tax + Subsidy
= (i) – (iii) – (ii) – (iv) + (v)
= 300 – 20 – (–4) – 30 + 5
= ₹ 259 Crores

NNP_{fc} = NDPfc + NFIA
= 259 + (–4)
= ₹ 255 Crores

PROBLEM–3:

Calculate Domestic Income (NDP_{fc})

	(₹ in Crore)
(i) GNPmp	6000
(ii) Subsidies	200
(iii) Depreciation	100
(iv) NFIA	400
(v) Indirect Taxes	300

Solution:

NDP_{fc} = GNPmp - Depreciation – NFIA – NIT
= (i) – (iii) – (iv) – (v – ii)
= 6000 – 100 – 400 – (300 – 200)
= ₹ 5400 Crores

PROBLEM–4:

Calculate NIT (Net Indirect Taxes)

	(₹ in Crore)
(i) GNP_{mp}	700
(ii) NDP_{fc}	620
(iii) Depreciation	60
(iv) NFIA	(– 40)

Solution:

NDP_{fc} = NDPfc = GNPmp – Depreciation – NFIA – NIT
(ii) = (i) – (iii) – (iv) – NIT
620 = 700 – 60 – (– 40) – NIT
NIT = ₹ 60 Crores

PROBLEM–5:

Calculate Consumption of Fixed Capital

	(₹ in Crore)
(i) National Income (NNP_{fc})	400
(ii) GDP_{mp}	500
(iii) NIT	30
(iv) NFIA	20

Solution:

Consumption of Fixed Capital

$$= ii - iii + iv - i$$
$$= 500 - 30 + 20 - 400$$
$$= ₹\ 90 \text{ Crores}$$

1.3 MEASUREMENT OF NATIONAL INCOME

One Mark Questions

Q. 1 State the classification of production units.

Ans.: Production units are classified into primary, secondary and territory sector.

Q. 2 What does primary sector consist of?

Ans.: It is a sector in which goods are produced by exploiting natural resources. These include agriculture, fishing, mining etc.

Q. 3 What does secondary sector consist of?

Ans.: It is a sector in which all production units are engaged in transforming one good into another.

It includes production units engaged in manufacturing, construction, electricity generation, water supply etc.

Q. 4 What does tertiary sector consist of?

Ans.: It is a sector in which all production units engaged in production of services. It includes services like communication, transport, trade finance etc.

Q. 5 Define value added. Give an example.

Ans.: It refers to the addition of value to the intermediate products by the production units.

For Example: If a baker use flour as intermediate product worth ₹ 1000 to transform it into bread and sell it for ₹ 1500. Then value added is ₹ 500 (1500 – 1000).

Q. 6 How is value added calculated?

Ans.: Value added (GVA_{mp}) = Value of Output – Intermediate Consumption

Q. 7 What is intermediate consumption?

Ans.: It refers to the use of intermediate products in the production process.

Q.8 How is value of output calculated?

Ans.: Value of output = Sales + Change in stock.

OR

(Quantity x Price) + Change in stock

Where change in stock = closing stock – opening stock

Q. 9 Define value added method.

Ans.: It refers to the measurement of national income in the different phases of production. It is also known as Production method, Net output method and Inventory method.

Q. 10 How is domestic product (GDPmp) calculated under value added method?

Ans.: Sum total of GVA_{mp} (Value added) of all sectors = GDP_{mp}

Q. 11 Define income distribution method.

Ans.: The method of measuring factor income which is distributed to the owners of factors of production by various industrial units is called income distribution method.

Q. 12 State the components of factor income.

Ans.: There are five components of factor income: –

(a) Compensation of employees.

(b) Rent and Royalty.

(c) Interest.

(d) Profit.

(e) Mixed Income of self-employed.

Q. 13 Define compensation of employees.

Ans.: It refers to total remuneration in cash on kind paid to employees by the employers for rendering productive services.

Q. 14 Define Rent.

Ans.: It is the amount payable by the tenants to the landlord.

Q. 15 Define Royalty.

Ans.: It is the amount payable to the landlord for granting leasing right of sub soil assets (like Coal, Iron Ore etc.).

Q. 16 Define Interest.

Ans.: It is the amount payable by the production unit for using borrowed money given by the owners.

Q. 17 Define Profit.

Ans.: It is a reward to an entrepreneur for his contribution in the production process.

Q. 18 What is mixed income?

Ans.: It is the income of self-employed, own account workers and profit, dividends of unincorporated enterprises.

Q. 19 Define operating surplus.

Ans.: It is the sum of rent, royalty, interest and profit.

Q. 20 State the three parts of profit.

Ans.: The three parts of profit are: –

1. Corporate Tax
2. Dividend
3. Retained earnings or Undistributed profits

Q. 21 Define corporate tax.

Ans.: It is the tax paid on the total profit earned by an enterprise to the government.

Q. 22 Define dividend.

Ans.: It is the part of the profit paid to the shareholders.

Q. 23 Define Retained Earnings or Undistributed Profits.

Ans.: It is the part of the profit kept as reserves.

Q. 24 Define final expenditure method.

Ans.: This method measures the expenditure incurred on final products produced by all production unit located within the economic territory during a given year.

Q. 25 State the components of Expenditure Method.

Ans.: The components of Expenditure Method are:

1. Private final consumption expenditure.
2. Government final consumption expenditure.
3. Gross domestic capital formation.
4. Net exports.

Q. 26 Define Private Final Consumption Expenditure (PFCE).

Ans.: It is the sum total of final consumption expenditure by households and private non-profit institutions serving households.

Q. 27 Define government final consumption expenditure (GFCE).

Ans.: It is the expenditure incurred by general government on providing various services.

Q. 28 Define Gross domestic capital formation (GDCF).

Ans.: It refers to the expenditure incurred by production units on acquiring goods for investment which are located within the domestic territory.

Q. 29 State the components of GDCF.

Ans.: It has two components: –

1. Gross fixed capital formation.
2. Net change in stock.

Q. 30 Define Gross fixed capital formation (GFCF).

Ans.: It refers to expenditure incurred on purchase of fixed assets.

Q. 31 State the sub categories of GFCF.

Ans.: Gross fixed capital formation is sub-divided into: –

1. Gross Business fixed investment (expenditure on purchase of machinery, equipments etc.).
2. Gross residential construction investment (Expenditure incurred on construction of new houses).
3. Gross public investment (expenditure on construction of flyovers, roads, bridges etc.).

Q. 32 Define net change in stock.

Ans.: It is the net addition to the stock of raw material, semi-finished goods and finished goods.

Q. 33 Define net exports.

Ans.: It is the difference between exports and imports of a country during a given period.

Q. 34 Why imports are deducted?

Ans.: Imports are deducted because a portion of PFCE, GFCE and GDCF consists of expenditure on imports. It is an expenditure on foreign products.

Q. 35 Why exports are included?

Ans.: Exports are included because it is an expenditure on domestic product by the foreigners which is a final expenditure.

3–4 Marks Questions

Q. 1 What are components of compensation of employees. Explain them.

Ans.: Compensation of employees has two components:

A. Wages and Salaries in cash and kind –

   (i) Wages and salaries in cash include wages, salaries, bonus, commission etc.

(ii) Wages and salaries in kind includes rent free accommodation, free medical treatment educational facilities etc.

B. Social security contribution by the employers like life insurance, labour welfare funds, gratuity, old age pension etc.

Q. 2 Explain the concept of mixed income.

Ans.: It means an income payment by production units which cannot be separable into separate heads (Rent, Interest, Royalty, Profit, compensation of employees).

It arises from productive service of self-employed persons, whose income includes wages, rent, interest and profit and these elements cannot be separated from each other.

For Example: Suppose if a doctor opens the clinic in his own building, invested his funds on machines etc. then he is the owner of land and entrepreneur as he has started his own clinic. He is also a worker while treating a patient. Thus, his income (i.e. rent, profit, interest etc.) cannot be separable into above heads as his income has elements of more than one type of factor income.

Q. 3 What is double counting? How it can be avoided?

Ans.: It is a problem of counting the value of certain goods and services more than once in the estimation of national income.

It can be avoided in two ways:

1. To take value added instead of total output. It means to take sum total of value added by each producing unit. This can be explained through the following example: –

Production Unit	***Value of Output***	–	***Intermediate Consumption***	=	***Value added***
Farmer	100	–	0	=	100
Baker	200	–	100	=	100
Grocer	**220**	–	200	=	20
	520	–	300	=	**220**

In the above example, the intermediate consumption of farmer is nil, and that of baker and grocer is a ₹ 100 and ₹ 200 respectively. Therefore, the sum total of value added by farmer, baker and grocer is ₹ 220.

2. To count only the value of final products. It means that value of only final goods should be added.

   In the above example.

Value of output i.e. only of grocer ₹ 220 is final product which is equal to sum total of value added by all the three production units.

6 Marks Questions

Q. 1 Explain the steps of value-added Method. what are its precautions?

Ans.: The various steps of value-added method are:

I. Classify all the production units into primary, secondary and tertiary sector.

II. Estimate NVAfc (net value added) of each industrial sector by taking the following steps:

1. Estimate value of output. i.e. value of output = Sales + Change in stock
2. Calculate GVAmp

   GVAmp = Value of output – Intermediate Consumption.
3. Calculate NVAmp

   NVAmp = GVAmp – Depreciation
4. Calculate NVAfc

   NVAfc= NVAmp– NIT

III. Take the sum of NVAfc of all industrial sectors of economy. i.e. $\Sigma NVA_{fc} = NDP_{fc}$ (Domestic Income).

IV. Add NFIA (net factor income from abroad) to NDP_{fc} to get national income.

i.e. NNP_{fc} (National Income) = NDP_{fc} (Domestic Income) + NFIA

The following precautions must be taken:

(1) Sale and purchase of second hand goods are not included because their values were counted in the year when they were produced.

(2) Value of intermediate goods is not included to avoid the problem of double counting.

(3) Domestic services like services of housewives etc. are not included as it is difficult to measure their market value.

(4) Production for self-consumption is included in national income as they contribute to the current output.

For Example: Output produced by farmers for self-consumption must be included.

(5) Imputed rental value of self-occupied house is included in national income.

(6) Value of services provided by the brokers and commission agents relating to sale and purchase of second hand goods is included in national income as they render productive services.

Q. 2 Explain the steps of Income. Distribution Method. What are its precautions.

Ans.: The various steps of Income Method are:

I. Classify the production units into primary, secondary and tertiary sector.

II. Estimate factor income paid out by each production unit which are:

(a) Compensation of employees.

(b) Rent and royalty.

(c) Interest.

(d) Profit.

(e) Mixed Income.

III. Take the sum of NVA_{fc} i.e., factor Income paid out by all production or industrial sector to get NDP_{fc}.

i. e.$\Sigma NVA_{fc} = NDP_{fc}$ (Domestic Income)

IV. Add NFIA (net factor income from abroad) to arrive at national income

i.e. NNP_{fc} (National Income) = NDP_{fc} (Domestic Income) + NFIA.

The following precautions must be taken:

(1) Transfer income like (scholarships, donation, charity etc.) are not included in national income as these are unilateral in nature i.e. receipts against which no goods and service are provided in return.

(2) Income from sale of second hands goods will not be included because it is not related to the current flow of goods and services.

(3) Incomes of gamblers, smugglers, thieves etc. is not included in national income because these are not the part of regular productive activities and are illegal activities.

(4) Income from safe of financial assets in the form of shares, bonds, debentures, government securities etc. will not be included as these are not related to production of goods and services in the current year.

(5) Income from windfall gains (like income from lottery, horse race etc.) are not included as these are not productive activities.

Q. 3 What are the steps of expenditure method? What are its precautions?

Ans.: The following steps of expenditure method are:

I. Classify production units into primary, secondary, tertiary sector.

II. Estimate final expenditure incurred by these production units into the following heads:

(i) Private final consumption expenditure (PFCE).

(ii) Government final consumption expenditure (GFCE).

(iii) Gross domestic capital formation (GDCF).

(iv) Net exports.

III. Take the sum of these heads to arrive at GDP_{mp}

i.e. GDP_{mp} = PFCE + GFCE + GDCF + Net Exports

IV. Calculate NDP_{fc} (domestic income). To calculate NDP_{fc} deduct consumption of fixed capital and NIT (net indirect taxes).

i.e. $NDP_{fc} = GDP_{mp}$ – Depreciation – NIT

V. Calculate NNP_{fc} (National Income). To calculate NNP_{fc} add NFIA (net factor income from abroad) to NDP_{fc} to arrive at NNP_{fc}.

i.e. NNP_{fc} (National Income) = NDP_{fc} (Domestic Income) + NFIA.

The following precautions of expenditures method are: –

(1) Expenditure on intermediate goods and services is not included in national income as it is already included in the value of final expenditure and it may create the problem of double counting.

(2) Expenditure on transfer payments (like donation, scholarships, charity etc.) is not included as these expenditures are not connected with production activities.

(3) Expenditure on purchase of financial assets (share, debentures, bonds etc.) will not be included as these expenditures are not related to production of goods and services in the current year.

(4) Expenditure on purchase of second hand goods will not be included as these goods are not a part of current flow of goods and services produced.

(5) Expenditure on own account production (e.g. production for selfconsumption, free services from general government or selfconsumed services of owner-occupied houses) will be included in national income as these are productive services.

Reconciliation of the three Method

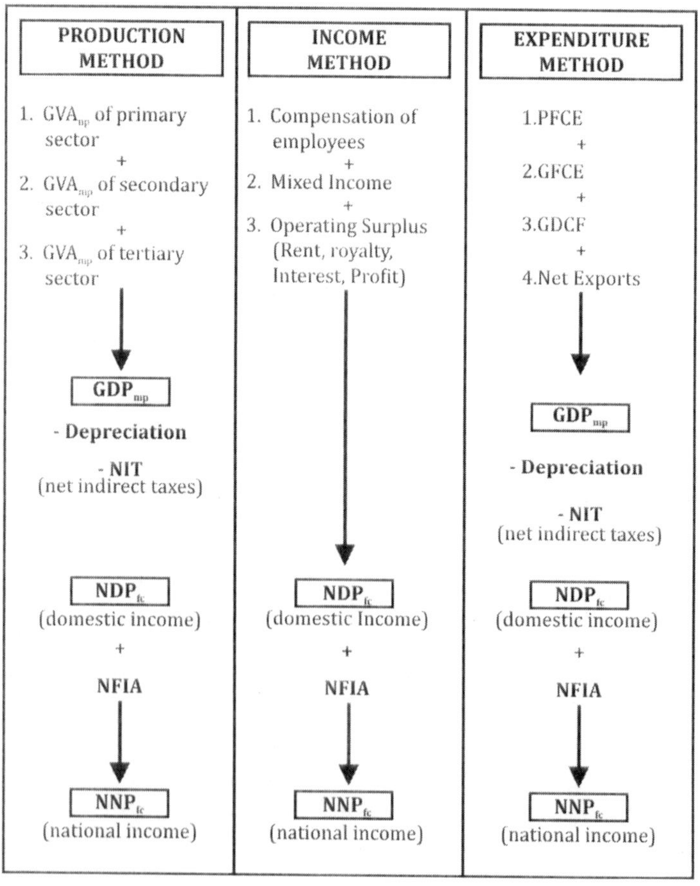

NOTE

A. (Value added by a production unit)

1.	GVA_{mp}	=	*Value of Output* ↓ (Sales + Change in Stock)	–	*Intermediate Consumption*
2.	NVA_{mp}	=	GVA_{mp} – depreciation		
3.	NVA_{fc}	=	NVA_{mp} – NIT		

B. GDCF (Gross Domestic Capital formation)

↙ Gross Fixed Capital Formation ↘ Net Change in Stock

Transactions Not Included in Estimation of National Income

Transaction	*Reason*
1. Sale and purchase of second hands goods, intermediate consumption expenditure.	It will lead to the problem of double counting. These are not a current production activity.
2. Transfer income and payments like pocket money, old age pension, scholarships etc.	These are not a current production activity.
3. Sale and purchase of financial assets like shares, debentures etc.	It does not lead to production of goods or a service. It is only a transfer of ownership.
4. Incomes from illegal activities like gambling, lottery etc.	These are not the result of a production activity.
5. Interest paid by consumer households, interest, received on general government loans.	Such borrowing is not used for production.
6. Services rendered by family member to each other.	Due to lack of data, values of these services are not included.

Transactions Included in Estimation of National income

Transaction	*Reason*
1. All expenditure made by the households, improvement of a fixed capital asset, school fees paid by students etc.	Included in national income through expenditure method.

(Contd...)

2. Compensation of employees like house rent allowance, medical expenses, allowances of member of parliament etc.	Included through income method.
3. Interest received by households from commercial banks, dividend received on shares, interest paid on debentures, payment of bonus to school employees etc.	Included through income method.
4. Commission on sale and purchase of second hand goods and brokerage paid on sale of financial assets.	These are given for carrying out the productive activity.
5. Expenditure on own account production (e.g. production for self-consumption, free services from general government, self-consumed services of owner-occupied houses) etc.	These are included through expenditure method and are productive services.
6. Profits earned by branch of an Indian bank abroad.	It is included as it to factor income from abroad.

SOLVED NUMERICALS (VALUE ADDED)

PROBLEM–1:

Calculate the GVA_{mp}

		(₹ in Lakh)
(i)	GST	40
(ii)	Closing Stock	20
(iii)	Sales	700
(iv)	Subsidy	5
(v)	Opening Stock	10
(vi)	Intermediate Consumption	400

Solution:

GVA_{mp} = iii + ii – v – vi

= 700 + 20 – 10 – 400

= ₹ 310 Lakh

PROBLEM–2:

Find out gross value added at market price	(₹ in Lakh)
(i) Depreciation	20
(ii) Domestic sales	200
(iii) Net change in stock	(–10)
(iv) Exports	10
(v) Single use producer goods	120

Solution:

$$\begin{aligned} \mathbf{GVA}_{mp} &= ii + iv + (iii) - v \\ &= 200 + 10 + (-10) - 120 \\ &= ₹\ 80 \text{ Lakh} \end{aligned}$$

PROBLEM–3:

Find out net value added at factor cost	**(₹ in Lakh)**
(i) Price per unit of output	25
(ii) Output sold (units)	1000
(iii) Excise duty	5000
(iv) Depreciation	1000
(v) Change in stock	(–500)
(vi) Intermediate cost	7000

Solution:

$$\begin{aligned} \mathbf{NVA}_{fc} &= (i \times ii) + v - vi - iv - iii \\ &= (25 \times 1000) + (-500) - 7000 - 1000 - 5000 \\ &= ₹\ 11500 \text{ Lakh} \end{aligned}$$

PROBLEM–4:

Calculate 'Sales' from the following data	**(₹ in Lakh)**
(i) NVA_{fc}	300
(ii) Intermediate consumption	200
(iii) Indirect tax	20
(iv) Depreciation	30
(v) Change in stock	(–50)

Solution:

$$\begin{aligned} \mathbf{Sales} &= (i + iv + iii) - (v - ii) \\ &= (300 + 30 + 20) - (-50 - 200) \\ &= 300 + 30 + 20 + 50 + 200 \\ &= ₹\ 600 \text{ Lakh} \end{aligned}$$

SOLVED NUMERICALS OF INCOME AND EXPENDITURE METHOD

Problem – 1:

Calculate GDP_{mp} and GNP_{mp}

		(₹)
(i)	Personal find consumption expenditure	52,000
(ii)	Government find consumption expenditure	5,000
(iii)	Gross domestic fixed capital formation	4,500
(iv)	Increase in inventories	600
(v)	Export of goods and services	800
(vi)	Import of goods and services	600
(vii)	Depreciation	600
(viii)	Net indirect taxes	2,000
(ix)	Net factor income from abroad	600

Solution:

GDP_{mp} = (i) + (ii) + (iii) + (iv) + (v) – (vi)

= 50000 + 5000 + 4500 + 600 + 800 – 600

= ₹ 62,300

GNP_{mp} = GDP_{mp} + (ix)

= 62300 + 600

= ₹ 62,900

Problem – 2

Calculate Gross domestic product at Market price from the following data

		(₹ in Crores)
(i)	Consumption of fixed capital	50
(ii)	Closing stock	40
(iii)	Private final consumption expenditure	500
(iv)	Opening Stock	60
(v)	Net factor income from abroad	(–35)
(vi)	Exports	25
(vii)	Government final consumption expenditure	200
(viii)	Imports	40
(ix)	Net Indirect taxes	100
(x)	Net domestic capital formation	300

Solution:

GDP_{mp} = iii + vii + (x + i) + (vi – viii)
= 500 + 200 + (300 + 50) + (25 – 40)
= ₹1035 Crores

Problem–3

From the following data calculate **(₹ in Crores)**

(a) Gross domestic product at factor cost

(b) Factor income to abroad

(i)	Compensation of employees	800
(ii)	Profits	200
(iii)	Dividends	50
(iv)	Gross National product at market price	1400
(v)	Rent	150
(vi)	Interest	100
(vii)	Gross domestic capital formation	300
(viii)	Net fixed capital formation	200
(ix)	Change in stock	50
(x)	Factor income from abroad	60
(xi)	Net indirect taxes	120

Solution:

GDP_{mp} = (i) + (ii) + (v) + (vi) + [vii – (viii + ix)]
= 800 + 200 + 150 + 100 + [300 – (200 + 50)]
= 800 + 200 + 150 + 100 + 50
= ₹ 1300 Crores

(b) Factor income to abroad

= x – [iv – (GDPfc + xi)]
= 60 – [1400 – (1300 + 120)]
= ₹ 80 Crores

Problem–4

Calculate national income and consumption of fixed capital

(₹ in Crores)

(i)	Private final consumption expenditure	210
(ii)	GDP_{mp}	320
(iii)	Wages and salaries	170
(iv)	Employer's contribution to provident fund	10

(v)	Interest	20
(vi)	Indirect taxes	30
(vii)	Subsidies	5
(viii)	Rent	10
(ix)	Profit	45
(x)	Royalty	15
(xi)	Net factor income from abroad	3

Solution:

National income (NNP_{fc})

= (iii) + (iv) + (v) + (viii) + (ix) + (x) + (xi)
= 170 + 10 + 20 + 10 + 45 + 15 + 3
= ₹ 273 Crores

Consumption of fixed capital

= GDP_{mp} + (xi) – (vi – vii) – NNP_{fc}
= 320 + 3 – (30 – 5) – 273
= ₹ 25 Crores

Problem–5

Calculate national income by income and expenditure method

		(₹ in Crores)
(i)	Private final consumption expenditure	2000
(ii)	Net capital formation	400
(iii)	Change in stock	50
(iv)	Compensation of employees	1900
(v)	Net exports	20
(vi)	Net indirect taxes	400
(vii)	Operating surplus	720
(viii)	Net factor income from abroad	(–20)
(ix)	Government final consumption expenditure	600
(x)	Consumption of fixed capital	100
(xi)	Employees contribution to social security schemes	100

Solution:

National income by income method

= (iv) + (vii) + (viii)
= 1900 + 720 + (–20)
= ₹ 2600 Crores

National income by expenditure method

= i + ix + ii + v + viii – (vi)
= 2000 + 600 + 400 + 20 + (–20) – 400
= ₹ 2600 crores

BOARD QUESTIONS

Q. 1 What is double counting? State any two approaches to correct the problem of double counting. (CBSE 2019, 2010).

Q. 2 What precautions should be taken while estimating national income by production method. (CBSE, Compt, 2015).

Q. 3 Define operating surplus. State its components (CBSE, Delhi 2003).

1.4 GDP AND WELFARE

ONE MARK QUESTIONS

Q. 1 Define real GDP or GDP at constant prices.

Ans.: When GDP of a given year is estimated on the basis of price of a base year it is called real GDP.

Q. 2 Define nominal GDP or GDP at current prices.

Ans.: When GDP of a given year is estimated on the basis of price of the current year or same year it is called nominal GDP.

Q. 3 How is real GDP calculated?

Ans.: $$\text{Real GDP} = \frac{\text{Nominal GDP}}{\text{Price Index}} \times 100$$

Q. 4 How is nominal GDP calculated?

Ans.: $$\text{Nominal GDP} = \frac{\text{Real GDP x Price Index}}{100}$$

Q. 5 What is per capita real GDP.

Ans.: It equals total real GDP divided by population.

Q. 6 What does per capita real GDP indicate?

Ans.: An increase in per capital real GDP indicate increase in per capita availability of goods and services.

Q. 7 What is GDP deflator?

Ans.: It is a price index that measures price inflation or deflation and is calculated using nominal GDP and real GDP.

$$\text{GDP Deflator} = \frac{\text{Nominal GDP}}{\text{Real GDP}} \times 100$$

Q. 8 Define welfare.

Ans.: It means the sense of wellbeing among the people.

Q. 9 What is economic welfare?

Ans.: Welfare affected by economic factors like income, consumption etc. is called economic welfare.

Q. 10 What is non-economic welfare?

Ans.: Welfare affected by non-economic factors like pollution, law and order etc. is called non-economic welfare.

Q. 11 What is social welfare?

Ans.: It refers to sum total of economic and non-economic welfare.

Q. 12 Define externalities.

Ans.: Activities which results in benefits or harms to others without any payment received for benefit and penalty for the harm done, such benefits and harms are called externalities.

Q. 13 What are positive externalities?

Ans.: Activities resulting in benefits to others are called positive externalities and it increases welfare.

Q. 14 What are negative externalities?

Ans.: Activities resulting in harms to others are called negative externalities and it decreases welfare.

3–4 Marks Questions

Q. 1 Distinguish between real GDP and nominal GDP.

Ans.:

Real GDP	*Nominal GDP*
1. It is estimated on the basis of price of base year	It is estimated on the basis of same year.
2. It is known as GDP at constant prices.	It is known as GDP at current prices.

(*Contd...*)

3. It is affected by change in physical output only.	It is affected by both change in price and physical output.
4. It is a real indicator of economic growth.	It is not a real indicator of economic growth.
5. Real GDP	Nominal GDP
$= \frac{\text{Nominal GDP}}{\text{Price Index}} \times 100$	$= \frac{\text{Real GDP} \times \text{Price Index}}{100}$

Q. 2 Distinguish between national income at constant prices and national income at current prices.

Ans.:

National Income at Constant Prices	*National Income at Current Price*
1. It refers to money value of final goods and services produced by normal residents of a country in a year measured at prices of base year.	It refers to money value of final goods and services produced by normal residents of a country in a year measured at price of current year.
2. It is known as real national income.	it is known as nominal national income.
3. It is a real indicator for measuring the economic growth of a country.	It is not a real indicator for measuring the economic growth of a country.
4. It is calculated at constant prices.	It is calculated at current year price.

$$\text{National Income at constant Price} = \frac{\text{National Income at Current Price}}{\text{Current Price Index}} \times 100$$

Q. 3 Explain how 'externalities' are a limitation of GDP as an indicator of welfare.

Ans.: Externalities refers to the various activities which results in harms or benefits. There is no penalty for harm done and no payment received for benefit.

- Negative Externalities refers to activities resulting in harms to other are:

  For Example: Pollution caused by industries in production of goods and services. Producing goods increases welfare but it creates pollution which reduces welfare.

- So, GDP does not take into account these negative externalities.

- Positive externalities refer to activities resulting in benefits to other.

  For Example: Public parks used by the people for morning walk, exercises etc.
- Expenditure on construction of public parks is included in GDP but not the benefits of public parks.
- Though public parks increase welfare as there will be positive effect on health of the people, yet it is not included as its value cannot be estimated.

Q. 4 Explain how 'non-monetary exchanges' a limitation of GDP as an index of welfare.

Ans.: There are many goods and services contributing economic welfare but not included in GDP.

For Example: Services of housewives, family members, leisure time activities etc. are not included in GDP, due to non-availability of data and their accurate valuation.

Q. 5 Explain how 'inequalities in income a limitation of GDP as an index of welfare.

Ans.: GDP does not take in account of changes in inequalities in the distribution of income.

- Inequality in the distribution of income may increase or decrease.
- If is increases; it implies that gap between the rich and poor increases.
- So, if welfare rises it may rise in less proportion as compared to rise in GDP.
- An increase in the GDP may be a result of the increase in the income of only a few individuals while the majority of people remain deprived of the benefits of the rise in the GDP. In such a situation, a rise in the GDP does not enhance the economic welfare.

Q. 6 All products may not contribute equally to economic welfare. Explain limitation of GDP as an index of welfare.

Ans.:

- Some products contribute more to the welfare of the people like food articles, clothes, houses etc. thus raising their standard of living.
- Some products like defence services etc. may contribute less to the welfare of the people but not directly affect the standard of living of the people.

- So economic welfare depends upon the types of goods and services produced and not how much is produced.
- So, welfare of the people may not rise as much as the rise in GDP.

Q. 7 "Contribution of some products may be negative". Explain this limitation of GDP as an index of welfare.

Ans.: GDP includes both healthy and harmful products consumed by the economy.

For Example: Milk and liquor. Consumption of milk leads to rise in welfare due to good effects on health. Liquor, when consumed, lead to decline in welfare due to harmful effect on health.

- GDP only includes their monetary values and not their contribution to welfare.
- Economic welfare depends upon the types of goods and services consumed.

Board Questions

Q. 1 Government spends on child immunization programme. Analyse its impact on gross domestic product and welfare of the people.

Q. 2 Government incurs expenditure to popularize Yoga among the masses. Analyze its impact on gross domestic product and welfare of the people.

(Hint: Yoga exercise improve health and thus raises efficiency of the people).

Q. 3 GDP does not give us a clear indication of economic welfare of a country. Defend or refute the given statement. (CBSE 2019).

Q. 4 Given nominal income, how can we find real income? Explain (CBSE 2018).

Q. 5 Define externalities. Give an example of negative externality. What is it impact on welfare (CBSE2014)?

Q. 6 If nominal GDP is ₹ 1200 and Price Index (with base ₹ 100) is ₹ 120, calculate Real GDP. (Hint Real GDP ₹ 1000). (CBSE 2015).

Unit – II

Money and Banking

2.1 Money and Money Supply

(i) Meaning of money.

(ii) Meaning of money supply.

(iii) Measures of money supply.

2.2 Banking

(i) Function of central Bank.

(ii) Definition of money multiplier.

(iii) Working of money multiplier.

1.1 MONEY AND MONEY SUPPLY

One Mark Questions

Q. 1 **Define money.**

Ans.: Money is defined as anything which is generally accepted as a medium of exchange, a store of value, a unit of account and a standard of deferred payment.

Q. 2 **Define money supply.**

Ans.: Money supply means currency with the public and demand deposits of banks at a given point of time.

OR

It is the stock of money on a specific day.

Q. 3 **State the components/measures (M1) of money supply.**

Ans.: The components of money supply are:

1. Currency with the public
2. Demand deposits

Q. 4 **Define high powered money.**

Ans.: It refers to currency which includes coins and currency notes and issued by RBI and Government.

Q. 5 **What is fiat money or currency?**

Ans.: It is defined as the money that the government declares as legal tender i.e. under law it must be accepted for all debts.

Q. 6 **What are demand deposits?**

Ans.: Bank deposits from which payment can be made by writing cheques. These are also called chequable deposits as such deposits can be encashed by issuing cheques at any time by the account holders.

3–4 Marks Questions

Q. 1 **Explain the measures/components of M1 of money supply.**

Ans.: The basic measure of money supply is transaction money (those assets which can be directly used for transactions). It consists of:

(i) Currency with public:

- It includes currency held outside the bank i.e. currency held only by public.
- It consists of paper notes and coins.

(ii) Demand deposits:

- These are the bank deposits from which payment can be made by writing cheques.
- There are two types of bank deposits i.e. time deposits and demand deposits. Time deposit are withdrawable only after a fixed period of time. e.g. Fixed deposits. But demand deposits can be encashed by issuing cheques at any time by the account holders.

Board Questions

Q. 1 **State any two components of M1 of money supply (CBSE 2019, 2017).**

Q. 2 **Define money supply. (CBSE 2018).**

Q. 3 **Define time deposits.**

Q. 4 **What are demand deposits? (CBSE 2014, 2013).**

2. 2 BANKING

One Mark Questions

Q. 1 **Define Bank.**

Ans.: Bank is a financial institution whose bank deposits are chequable and has the power to create money.

Q. 2 **List two characteristics functions which banks perform while other financial institutions do not perform.**

Ans.: The two characteristics are:

1. Bank deposits are chequable.
2. Bank create money.

Q. 3 **What is a structure of banking system?**

Ans.: A banking structure consists of:

1. Central bank (Reserve Bank of India).
2. Commercial Banks (State Bank of India, Axis Bank etc.).

Q. 4 **Define central bank.**

Ans.: It is an apex institution which controls and regulates the banking and monetary system of a country and has the sole authority for the issue of currency of that country.

Q. 5 Define commercial bank.

Ans.: It is an institution that accepts deposits from the people and extends loans and advance to them to create money.

Q. 6 Define money multiplier or deposit multiplier.

Ans.: The multiple by which banks can create deposits due to an initial deposit is called money multiplier or deposit multiplier. It is determined by LRR (Legal Reserve Ratio).

Q. 7 What is formula of deposit multiplier and total deposit.

Ans.: 1. Deposit Multiplier = 1/LRR (Legal Reserve Ratio).

2. Total Deposit = Initial deposit x money multiplier.

Q. 8 Define LRR (Legal reserve Ratio).

OR

Define required reserve ratio, reserve deposit ratio.

Ans.: It is a certain minimum fraction of deposit, which is legally compulsory for the commercial banks to keep in the form of liquid assets or cash.

Q. 9 State the components of LRR.

Ans.: It has two components:

1. SLR (Statutory Liquidity Ratio)
2. CRR (Cash Reserve Ratio)

Q. 10 Define statutory liquidity ratio (SLR).

Ans.: It is a ratio of deposits which banks have to keep with themselves as reserves.

Q. 11 Define cash reserve ratio (CRR).

Ans.: It is the ratio of deposits which commercial banks have to keep with central bank as reserve.

Q. 12 What are the main instruments used by the central bank in performing its controller of credit function?

Ans.: The main instruments are:

(i) Open market operations
(ii) CRR
(iii) SLR
(iv) Repo Rate
(v) Reverse Repo Rate
(vi) Margin Requirement
(vii) Moral Suasion

Q. 13 What are quantitative instruments?

Ans.: Quantitative instruments include open market operations, CRR, SLR, repo rate, reverse repo rate.

Q. 14 What are qualitative instruments?

Ans.: Qualitative instruments include margin requirements and moral suasion.

Q. 15 Define open market operations.

Ans.: It refers to buying and selling of securities by the central bank in the open market.

Q. 16 Define repo rate (RR).

Ans.: It is the interest rate at which the commercial banks can borrow from the central bank to meet their short-term needs.

- In India its duration is up to 7 days.

Q. 17 Define reverse repo rate (RRR).

Ans.: It is the interest rate at which the commercial banks can deposit their funds with the central bank.

Q. 18 Define bank rate (discount rate).

Ans.: It is the interest rate at which the commercial banks can borrow from the central bank to meet their long-term needs.

Q. 19 Define margin requirements.

Ans.: It is the discount fixed by the central bank on the security mortgaged by the borrower to the commercial banks.

Q. 20 Define moral suasion.

Ans.: When central bank gives oral or written advice to the commercial banks for expanding or restrict credit it is called moral suasion.

Q. 21 Define 'controller of credit' as a function of central bank, what is the main objective.

Ans.: It refers to the legal power of the central bank to influence credit creation. Its main objective to minimize the fluctuation in general price level.

3–4 Marks Questions

Q. 1 Explain 'Bank of issue' as the function of central bank.

Ans.: Bank of Issue (Currency Authority).

- Bank has the exclusive authority to issue the currency.

- RBI (Reserve Bank of India) has the legal right to issue currency notes.
- The monopoly power of note issue is given to the central bank because of
  1. It brings uniformity in note circulation.
  2. It also gives power to the central bank to direct control over the money supply.

Q. 2 Explain 'Banker, agent, advisor to the government' as the function of central bank.

Ans.: As a Banker, Central Bank provides all services and facilities to the government like commercial banks provide services to the public.

- It manages all government department undertaking and funds of the government.
- It provides loans to the government in the situation of excess expenditure over revenue.
- It carries out their inter banking transactions and other banking operations.

As an Agent, central bank manages public debt. It undertakes all sorts of services relating to public debt.

As an advisor, central bank advises the government on economic policy matter, on capital and money market issues etc.

Q. 3 Explain Banker's Bank and Supervisor' as the function of Central Bank.

Ans.: (A) Banker's Bank or custodian of cash reserves,

- The central bank maintains the cash reserves of commercial banks.
- Every commercial bank has to keep a certain percent of its cash reserves with the central bank.
- Thus, central bank acts as a custodian.

II. Lender of Last Resort

- Central bank, is under the obligation to provide funds against securities to the commercial bank as and when needed by them.
- When a commercial bank faces financial crisis and fails to fulfill their requirements from other sources, central bank provides them with the financial assistance in the

form of credit. Thus, central bank plays the role of lender of last resort.

III. Clearing Agent

- All commercial banks have their accounts with the central bank.
- So, it become easier for central banks to settle various claims of commercial banks against each other.

(B) As a Supervisor

- The whole functioning of commercial banks is regulated and controlled by the central bank.
- The control is exercised by periodic inspection of banks.
- It also undertakes various issues regarding licensing, branch expansion, management, winding up etc.

Q. 4 How does central bank control availability of credit by open market operations?

Ans.: Open market operations refer to buying and selling of securities by the central bank in the open market.

- When central bank wants to control the volume of credit, it starts selling securities to the open market.
- It reduces the cash reserves of the commercial banks.
- This in turn reduces the credit creation capacity of the commercial banks.

Q. 5 Explain the effect of buying of securities in the open market?

Ans.: When central bank wants to increase the volume of credit, it starts buying securities from the open market.

- It increases the case reserves of the commercial banks.
- This in turn increases the lending capacity of the commercial banks.

Q. 6 Explain the effect of increase in CRR (Cash Reserve Ratio) by Central Bank.

Ans.: It is the ratio of deposit which commercial banks have to keep with central bank as reserves.

During inflation, Central Bank increases the CRR to reduce excess reserves of commercial banks and thus reducing their lending capacity.

Q. 7 Explain the effect of 'decrease' in CRR by Central Bank.

Ans.: To check deflationary tendencies in economy central bank, lower the CRR to increase the reserves of commercial banks. Thus, it raises their lending capacity.

Q. 8 Explain the effect of changes in SLR on money supply.

Ans.: It is the ratio of deposits which the commercial banks have to keep with themselves as reserves.

- During inflation, central bank increases the SLR to reduce excess reserves of commercial banks and reducing their lending capacity.
- During deflation, central bank decreases the SLR to increase the reserves of commercial banks.
- Thus, it raises their lending capacity.

Q. 9 Explain the effect of changes in repo rate (RR) on money supply?

Ans.: It is the interest rate at which the commercial banks can borrow from the central banks to meet their short-term needs.

- During inflation, central bank, raises it which increases the cost of borrowing for the commercial banks.
- Commercial banks are forced to raise their lending rates which discourages borrowers from taking loans.
- Thus, it reduces the ability of banks to create credit.
- During deflation, central bank lower it which decreases the cost of borrowings from the central bank.
- Commercial banks also lower their lending rates which encourages borrowers for taking loans.
- Thus, it increases the ability of various bank to create credit.

Q. 10 Explain the effect of changes in bank rate on money supply?

Ans.: It is the interest rate at which the commercial banks can borrow from the central bank to meet their long-term needs.

- During inflation, it raises it which increases the cost of borrowings for the commercial banks.
- Commercial bank raises their lending rate which discourages borrowers from taking loans.
- Thus, it reduces the ability to create credit.
- During deflation, its lower bank rate which decreases the cost of borrowings for various banks.
- Commercial bank lowers their lending rates for providing more loans.
- Thus, it increases the ability to create credit.

OR

Explain ro... repo rate in contro... (CBSE 2017, 20...

Q. 3 **Explain how open market operations are helpful in controlling credit creation. (CBSE 2016).**

Q. 4 **Government of India has recently launched 'Jan DhanYojna' aimed at every household to have atleast one bank account in the country. Explain how deposits made under the plan are going to affect national income of the country. (CBSE 2015).**

Ans.:

- Opening more bank accounts means more bank deposits.
- More deposits mean increase in the lending capacity.
- More lending by banks means more investment in the country.
- More investment means more national income.

Q. 5 **Explain 'lender of last resort' function. (CBSE 2018, 2014, 2013)**

Q. 6 **Explain the credit creation of role of commercial banks with the help of a numerical example. (CBSE 2013)**

Q. 7 **Currency is issued by the central bank, yet we say that commercial banks create money. Explain. How is this money creation likely to affect the national income? (CBSE 2015)**

Ans.: Commercial banks create deposits by lending money to the investors. The rise in investment in the economy leads to rise in national income through the multiplier effect.

co[ans so the ...
gi back to the bank in form ... customers will turn ...
assumed that not all customers will ... commercial banks keep a p...
withdraw their deposits so commercial banks keep a p...
f deposits as reserves and lend the rest.

- Thus, there is constant flow of new deposits into the bank.
- The process of creation of money is explained with the help of numerical example.

Money Multiplier Table

Rounds	Deposit Received	Loans	Reserves (LRR 20%)
Initial	10,000	8,000	2,000
I	8,000	6,400	1,600
II	6,400	5,120	1,280
–	–	–	–
n^{th} Round	–	–	–
Total:	₹50,000	₹40,000	₹10,000

- Initially public deposit is ₹ 10,000 and LRR – 20 percent .
- It means that banks keep only ₹ 2000 as reserves and lend the remaining amount of ₹ 8000 by opening the accounts in the names of the borrowers. This is the first-round creation and equals 80 percent of initial deposit.
- Since all the transactions are routed through the banks, the money spent by the borrowers come back into the banks into the deposit accounts of those who have received the payment. this increases demand deposit by ₹ 8000.
- Now out of new deposits of ₹ 8000 the bank will keep 20 percent as reserve (i.e ₹ 1600) and lend the remaining amount (i.e. ₹ 6400).
- Again, this money will come back to the bank and this again increases demand deposit by ₹ 6400.
- The same process continues and with each round the total deposits with the bank's increases.
- The process comes to an end when total cash reserves become equal to initial deposit. So as per example, with the initial deposits of ₹10000, the commercial banks have created money of ₹ 50000.

Unit – III

Determination of Income and Employment

3. 1 Basic Concepts

(i) Aggregate demand and its components.
(ii) Aggregate supply.
(iii) Concepts of Propensity to Consume and Propensity to Save.

3. 2 Theory of Income Determination

(i) Consumption function and Saving function.
(ii) Derivation.
(iii) Equilibrium through Aggregate Demand and Aggregate Supply approach Saving and Investment Approach.
(iv) Multiplier and relation with MPC and MPS.
(v) Working of an investment multiplier.

3. 3 Excess Demand and Deficient Demand

(i) Inflationary Gap (Excess Demand).
(ii) Deflationary Gap (Deficient Demand).
(iii) Measures to correct excess demand and deficient demand.

3.1 BASIC CONCEPTS

One Mark Questions

Q. 1 Define Aggregate Demand (AD).

Ans.: It refers to the total ex-ante (planned) expenditure on final goods and services in an economy at a given level of income during a period of time.

Q. 2 State the components of aggregate demand.

Ans.: The components of aggregate demand are:

(i) Private consumption expenditure.

(ii) Investment expenditure.

(iii) Government expenditure.

(iv) Net exports.

Q. 3 Define Aggregate Supply (AS).

Ans.: It refers to value of final goods and services planned to be produced by all the producers in an economy in a given time period.

Q. 4 Why is AS equals to national income?

Ans.: AS is equals to national income because it is the production of output that generator income (rent, interest, profit, wages) to the factors of production.

AS = National Output = National Income

Q. 5 State the components of Aggregate Supply.

Ans.: Its components are:

(i) Consumption

(ii) Saving

AS = C + S

(Aggregate Supply) = (Consumption) + (Saving)

OR

National Income (Y) = C + S

Y = AS = C + S

Q. 6 Define propensity to consume.

Ans.: Propensity to consume means the proportion of income spent on consumption.

Q. 7 State the measures of propensities to consume.

Ans.: There are two types:

(i) Average Propensity to Consume (APC)

(ii) Marginal Propensity to Consume (MPC)

Q. 8 Define average propensity to consume (APC).

Ans.: It is defined as the ratio of total consumption expenditure to total income.

$$APC = \frac{\text{Total Consumption Expenditure}}{\text{Total Income}} = \frac{C}{Y}$$

Q. 9 Value of APC can be greater than one. Give reason.

Ans.: The value of APC can be greater than one. It is possible when at very low level of income consumption expenditure cannot fall below a minimum level.

For Example: When income is ₹ 200 and minimum level of consumption ₹ 220 then –

$$APC = \frac{220}{200} = 1.1$$

Q. 10 When is the value of APC equal to one?

Ans.: APC = 1 when consumption is equal to income.

Q. 11 Why the value of APC can never be zero?

Ans.: The value of APC can never be zero because consumption cannot be zero.

Q. 12 When is the value of APC is less than 1?

Ans.: This happens when consumption expenditure is less than national income.

Q. 13 Define marginal propensity to consume (MPC).

Ans.: It refers to ratio of change in consumption expenditure to change in income.

$$MPC = \frac{\text{Change in Consumption Expenditure}}{\text{Change in Income}} = \frac{\Delta C}{\Delta Y}$$

Suppose income rises from '₹ 1000 to '₹ 1200 and consumption rises from '₹ 800 to '₹ 850, then

$$MPC = \frac{\Delta C}{\Delta Y} = \frac{50}{200} = .25$$

Q. 14 Value of MPC can vary from zero to one but cannot be greater than one. Give reason.

Ans.: Value of MPC is equal to one when entire additional income is spent on consumption.

Value of MPC is equal to zero when entire additional income is saved.

Value of MPC cannot be greater than one because change in consumption cannot be more than change in income

Q. 15 Define propensity to save.

Ans.: Propensity to save is the proportion of income saved.

Q. 16 State the measure of propensity to save.

Ans.: The two measures are:

(i) Average Propensity to Save (APS).

(ii) Marginal Propensity to Save (MPS).

Q. 17 Define Average Propensity to Save (APS).

Ans.: It refers to ratio of total saving to total income.

$$\text{APC} = \frac{\text{Total Savings}}{\text{Total Income}} = \frac{\text{S}}{\text{Y}}$$

Q. 18 When is the value of APS be negative?

Ans.: Value of APS can be negative when at very low level of income. Consumption expenditure exceeds income.

For Example: At an income level of ₹ 200, consumption expenditure is '₹ 220 then,

$$\text{Saving} = \text{Income} - \text{Consumption}$$

$$\text{Saving} = 200 - 220$$

$$= -20$$

$$\text{So, APS} = \frac{-20}{200} = -0.1$$

Q. 19 Why is value of APS can never be more or equal to one?

Ans.: This is because savings can never be more or equal to income.

Q. 20 Define marginal propensity to save (MPS).

Ans.: It refers to the ratio of change in saving to change in income.

$$\text{MPS} = \frac{\text{Change in Saving}}{\text{Change in Income}} = \frac{\Delta \text{S}}{\Delta \text{Y}}$$

Q. 21 Why is the value of MPS varies from zero to one?

Ans.: MPS is equal to zero when entire additional income is spent on consumption i.e. saving is zero.

MPS is equal to one when the entire additional income is saved.

Q. 22 What is the relationship between APC and APS

Ans.:

$$APC + APS = 1$$

$$= \frac{C}{Y} + \frac{S}{Y} = 1$$

$$= \frac{C + S}{Y} \left(\frac{\text{Consumption} + \text{Saving}}{\text{Income}}\right) = \frac{Y}{Y} = 1$$

Q. 23 What is the relationship between MPC and MPS?

Ans.:

$$MPC + MPS = 1$$

$$\frac{\Delta C}{\Delta Y} + \frac{\Delta S}{\Delta Y}$$

$$= \frac{\Delta C + \Delta S}{\Delta Y}$$

$$= \frac{\Delta Y}{\Delta Y} = 1$$

Q. 24 Define full employment.

Ans.: It refers to a situation in which all those who are able and willing to work at given wage rate gets work.

Q. 25 Define Involuntary unemployment.

Ans.: It refers to a situation in which all those who are able and willing to work do not get work.

Q. 26 Define voluntary unemployment.

Ans.: It refers to a situation in which all those people who prefers not to work even though suitable work is available for them.

Q. 27. Define ex-ante and ex-post.

Ans.: Ex-ante means planned.

Ex-post means realized.

3–4 Marks Questions

Q. 1 Explain the components of AD.

Ans.: The components of AD are:

1. **Private consumption expenditure** – It refers to planned expenditure on final goods and services by all the households during an accounting year.
    - It depends upon the level of disposable income.
2. **Investment expenditure** – It refers to planned expenditure on capital goods by all the producers during a period of time.
    - Capital goods include building, equipment, machinery etc.
    - It is influenced by the rate of interest.
3. **Government expenditure** – It refers to planned expenditure on providing free services to the people through government.
    - Free services like law and order, education, health, defence, roads, highways etc.
    - It depends upon the policy of the government which is guided by the motive of social welfare.
4. **Net Exports** – It refers to planned net expenditure by the foreigners on the goods and services produced in the country during a period of time.
    - It depends upon rate of exchange, trade policy, terms of trade etc.

Q. 2 Distinguish between APC and MPC.

Ans.:

	APC	*MPC*
1.	It is the ratio of total consumption expenditure to total income.	It is the ratio of change in consumption expenditure to change in income.
2.	Its value can be more than one or less than 1.	Its value varies from zero to one.
3.	$APC = \frac{C}{Y}$	$MPC = \frac{\Delta C}{\Delta Y}$

Q. 3 Distinguish between APS and MPS

Ans.:

APS	*MPS*
It refers to ratio of total saving to total income.	It refers to ratio of change in saving to change in income.
Its value can be less than zero i.e. APS is negative.	Its value varies from zero to one.
$APS = \frac{S}{Y}$	$MPS = \frac{\Delta S}{\Delta Y}$

Basic formulae at a Glance:

1. $APC = \frac{C}{Y}$, $APS = \frac{S}{Y}$

2. $MPC = \frac{\Delta C}{\Delta Y}$, $MPS = \frac{\Delta S}{\Delta Y}$

3. APC + APS = 1, MPC + MPS = 1

Numericals

Problem–1:

Complete the following table.

Income	*Saving*	*MPC*	*APC*
0	– 12		
20	– 6		
40	0		
60	6		

Solution:

Income	*Saving*	*Consumption* $C = Y - S$	*MPC*	*APC*
0	– 12	12	–	–
20	– 6	26	0.70	– 0.30
40	0	40	0.70	0
60	6	54	0.70	0.10

Problem–2:

From the following schedule calculate APC, APS, MPC and MPS.

Income	50	100	150	200
Saving	10	40	75	120

Solution:

Income	*Saving*	*Consumption*	*APC*	*APS*	*MPC*	*MPS*
50	10	40	0.80	0.20	–	–
100	40	60	0.60	0.40	0.40	0.60
150	75	75	0.50	0.50	0.30	0.70
200	120	80	0.40	0.60	0.10	0.90

BOARD QUESTIONS

Q. 1 What is meant by aggregate demand? State its components. (CBSE 2019, 2018).

Q. 2 Give the meaning of involuntary unemployment. (CBSE 2017).

Q. 3 Distinguish between marginal propensity to consume and average propensity to consume. Give a numerical example. (CBSE 2016).

Q. 4 Complete the following table.

Income	*Consumption Expenditure*	*Marginal Propensity to Save*	*Average Propensity Save*
0	80	–	–
100	140	0.4	–
200	–	–	0
–	240	–	0.20
–	260	0.8	0.35

Solution:

Income	*C*	*S*	*MPS* $\left(\frac{\Delta S}{\Delta Y}\right)$	*APS* $\left(\frac{S}{Y}\right)$
0	80	– 80	–	–
100	140	– 40	0.4	– 0.4
200	200	0	0.4	0
300	240	60	0.6	0.20
400	260	140	0.8	0.35

3.2 THEORY OF INCOME DETERMINATION

ONE MARK QUESTIONS

Q. 1 State the assumptions of theory of income determination.

Ans.: The assumptions of theory of income determination are:

1. It is a short run analysis.
2. Price level is assumed to be fixed in the economy.
3. The economy is a closed economy.
4. There is no government expenditure.

Q. 2 Define closed economy.

Ans.: A closed economy is that economy which has no economic relations with the rest of the world.

Q. 3 What is autonomous variable?

Ans.: Autonomous variable is the variable which is not affected by national income.

Q. 4 What is an induced variable?

Ans.: Induced variable is the variable which an affected by national income.

Q. 5 Define consumption function.

Ans.: It refers to relation between consumption expenditure and income.

Q. 6 Define saving function.

Ans.: It refers to relation between income and saving.

Q. 7 What is the significance of 45° line?

Ans.: AS is represented by the 45° line. A comparison of consumption curve with 45° line shows that whether consumption expenditure is equal to, greater than or less than the level of income.

Q. 8 Define break even point.

Ans.: The point where consumption expenditure is equal to income.

Q. 9 State the two approaches for determining the equilibrium level of income.

Ans.: The two approaches are:

(i) AD and AS approach.

(ii) Saving and Investment approach.

Q. 10 What is AD and AS approach?

Ans.: According to this approach, the national income is in equilibrium at a point where AD is equal to AS.

Q. 11 What is saving and investment approach.

Ans.: It according to this approach, national income is in equilibrium at a point where planned saving equals planned investment.

Q. 12 Define full employment income level?

Ans.: It is the level that can be achieved when resources in the economy are fully employed.

Q. 13 Define full employment level of equilibrium.

Ans.: it refers to a situation when aggregate demand is equal to the aggregate supply at full employment level.

Q. 14 Define under employment equilibrium.

Ans.: It is a situation when aggregate demand is equal to aggregate supply at less than full employment level of income.

Q. 15 Define multiplier or investment multiplier.

Ans.: It refers to increase in national income as a multiple of given increase in investment.

Q. 16 How can we measure multiplier?

Ans.: It is the ratio of change in income to change in investment.

$$K \text{ (multiplier)} = \frac{\Delta Y \text{ (Change in income)}}{\Delta I \text{ (Change in investment)}}$$

Q. 17 State the relationship of MPC with multiplier.

Ans.:
- There is a direct relationship between MPC and multiplier.
- Higher the value of MPC, higher will be the value of multiplier.

$$K = \frac{1}{1\text{-MPC}}$$

Q. 18 State the relationship of MPS with multiplier.

Ans.:
- There is an inverse relationship between the value MPS and multiplier.
- Lower the value of MPS, higher will be the value of multiplier.

$$K = \frac{1}{MPS}$$

Q. 19 What is the minimum value of multiplier?

Ans.: Minimum value of multiplier is one when value of MPC is zero.

$$\text{i.e. } K = \frac{1}{1 - MPC}$$

$$K = \frac{1}{1 - 0} = 1.$$

Q. 20 What is the maximum value of multiplier?

Ans.: Maximum value of multiplier is infinity when value of MPC is one.

$$\text{i.e. } K = \frac{1}{1 - MPC}$$

$$K = \frac{1}{1 - 1} = \frac{1}{0} = \text{infinity}$$

3–4 Marks Questions

Q. 1 What is the equation of consumption function? Explain it.

Ans.: The equation of consumption function is expressed as:

$$C = \overleftarrow{C} + by$$

Where C = Total Consumption Expenditure

$\overleftarrow{C}$ = Autonomous Consumption

It means that consumption expenditure is not affected by change in income. i.e. at zero level of income there is some level of consumption expenditure.

b = MPC and Y = Income

MPC or (b) shows how consumption expenditure changes with changes in income. This portion of consumption is called as induced consumption.

Induced Consumption = MPC x Income

Q. 2 What is the equation of saving function? Explain it.

Ans.: The equation of saving function is expressed as:

$$S = -\overleftarrow{C} + (1 - b)\ y$$

Where – C = amount of negative saving at zero level of income.

1 – b = MPS

Y = Income

6 MARKS QUESTIONS

Q. 1 Explain the derivation of saving curve from consumption curve. Shown on a diagram when APC = 1, APS = 0 and APS is negative.

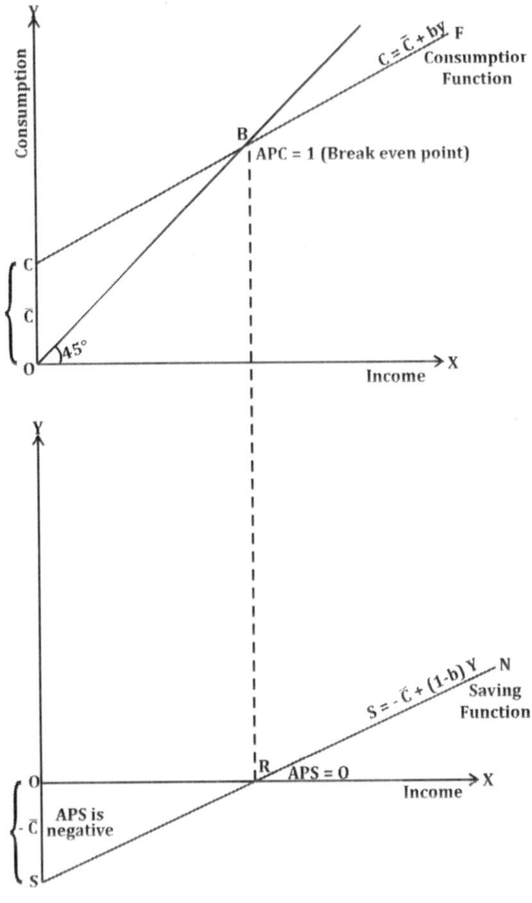

Explanation of Consumption Curve

- CF is the consumption curve which starts from point C as it indicates autonomous consumption.
- Each point on this curve shows the income and expenditure combination.
- 45° line represents that whether consumption expenditure is greater, equal or less than level of income.

- B is the break-even point where consumption expenditure is equal to income i.e. a point where APC = 1.
- To the left of point B, consumption expenditure is more than income (C >Y) i.e. dissaving.
- To the right of point B, consumption expenditure is less than income i.e. it shows saving.

Derivation

1. Draw a perpendicular from point B on consumption curve intersecting X-axis at point R where saving is zero.
2. Take OS part i.e. ($-\overleftarrow{C}$) equal to OC i.e. ($\overleftarrow{C}$) on Y axis.
3. This is the point from where the saving curve will start.
4. Now, joining the points S and R and extending this straight line further upwards, we get the saving curve SRN.

Q. 2 Derive the consumption curve from saving curve.

Ans.:

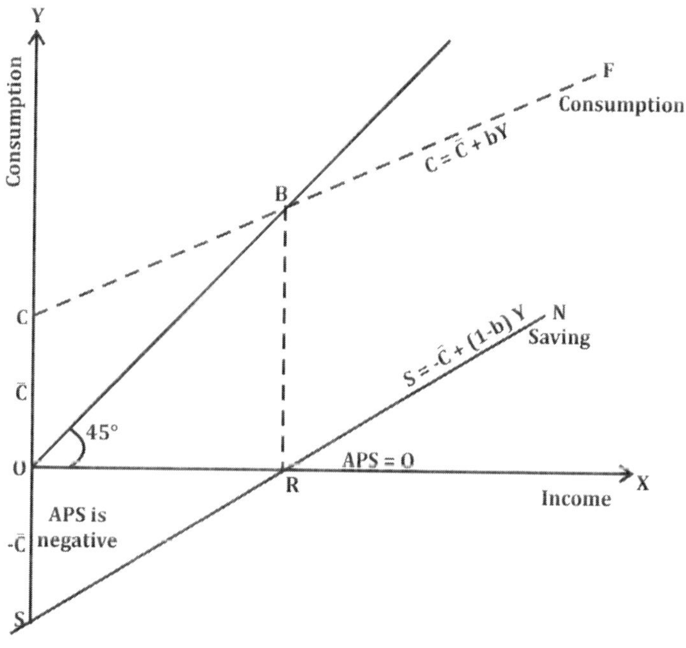

Explanation of the saving curve

- SN is the saving curve which starts from point S.
- Point S shows that there are amount of negative saving at zero level of income i.e. $-\overleftarrow{C}$ which is shown by OS.

- At point R saving are zero i.e. APS = O.

Steps of derivation

(1) Draw a 45° line from the origin.

(2) Take OC part equal to OS on Y axis.

(3) C is the point showing starting point of consumption curve. OC part shows autonomous consumption.

(4) Now draw a perpendicular from point R which intersects the 45° line at point B.

(5) Join point C and B and extend it upwards to get the consumption curve.

Q. 3 What happens to the level of national income when (i) AD is less than AS and (ii) AD is more than AS. Explain it with the help of schedule and diagram.

Ans.: The equilibrium level of national income is determined at the point where AD is equal to AS.

- AD is represented by C+I as there is neither foreign trade nor government.
- Consumption expenditure rises with the level of income and investment is autonomous not influenced by the level of income.
- As curve is represent by C+S curve. Which is depicted by a 45° line.

In the given schedule

- Value of MPC is 0.50.
- Investment all levels of income is '₹ 50 crore.

Equilibrium by AD and AS approach

(₹ Crore)

Income	*Consumption*	*Saving*	*Investment*	*AD (C+I*	*AS (C+S)*	*Remarks*
0	50	–50	50	100	0	AD > AS
50	75	–25	50	125	50	AD > AS
100	100	0	50	150	100	AD > AS
200	150	50	50	200	200	AD = AS
300	200	100	50	250	300	AD < AS
400	250	150	50	300	400	AD < AS
500	300	200	50	350	500	AD < AS
600	350	250	50	450	600	AD < AS

In the above schedule AD = AS at equilibrium level of income i.e. '₹ 200 crore.

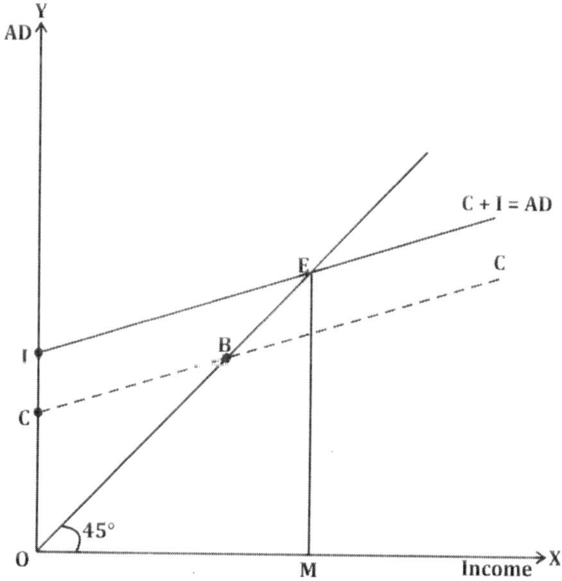

- In the diagram equilibrium is at point E where AD = AS.
- Equilibrium income level is OM.
- Adding investment to C curve, we get AD curve i.e. (C + I) which is parallel to C curve.

I. What happens when AD is less than AS.

Ans.: It means that consumers are planning to buy less goods than firms are planning to produce.

- This led to a situation of excess inventory.
- As a result, the producers will cut down the production which will reduce the income level i.e. AS.
- This will go on till AD and AS once again become equal.
- This brings the economy back to equilibrium.

II. What happens when AD is more than AS.

- It means that consumers are planning to buy more goods than firms are planning to produce.
- This led to fall in the level of inventory.
- As a result, producers will increase the production to meet the excess demand.

- This will raise national income i.e. AS.
- This will go on till AD and AS once again becomes equal.
- This brings the economy back to equilibrium.

Q. 5 Explain the equilibrium through saving investment approach explaining the situations.

1. When planned savings are more than planned investment.
2. When planned savings are less than planned investment. Also prepare schedule and diagram.

Ans.: According to the approach, the equilibrium level of income is determined at a level where planned saving is equal to planned investment.

- Investment is parallel to X-axis as it is an autonomous investment.
- Saving curve slopes upwards showing that as income rises, saving also rises.

Equilibrium by Saving and Investment Approach

(₹ Crore)

Income	*Consumption*	*Saving*	*Investment*	*Change in Inventory (S – I)*	*Remarks*
0	50	–50	50	– 100	S < I
50	75	–25	50	– 75	S < I
100	100	0	50	– 50	S < I
200	150	50	50	0	S = I
300	200	100	50	50	S > I
400	250	150	50	100	S > I
500	300	200	50	150	S > I
600	350	250	50	200	S > I

In the above schedule

- **Autonomous consumption is ₹ 50 Crore.**
- **Value of MPC is 0.50.**

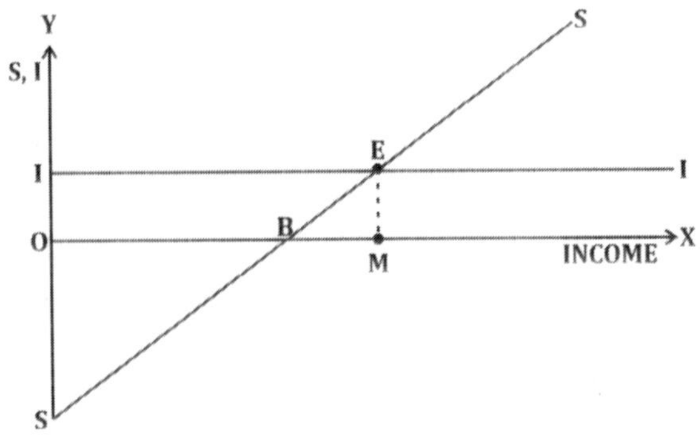

- Autonomous investment is ₹ 50 Crore.
- In the diagram equilibrium is at point E where S = I.
- Equilibrium level of income is OM.
- Saving curve is SS.
- Investment is autonomous.

I. What happens when planned savings are more than planned investments?

- It is a situation when AD is less than AS.
- It means that consumers are planning to buy less goods than firms are planning to produce.
- This led to excess inventory.
- As a result, the producers will cut down the production and inventory level will fall.
- It will reduce the income level i.e. AS and this will go on till saving and investment become equal to each other.

II. When planned saving are less than planned investment.

- It is a situation when AD is more than AS.
- It means that consumers are planning to buy more goods than firms are planning to produce.
- This results in fall in the inventory level.
- Producers will increase the production and inventory level will rise.
- It will increase the income level i.e. AS.
- This process will go on till saving and investment become equal to each other.
- This brings the economy back to the equilibrium.

Q. 6 Explain the working of multiplier with the help of a numerical example.

Ans.: Multiplier refers to increase in national income as a multiple of given increase in investment.

$$K = \frac{\Delta Y}{\Delta I}$$

Total increase in income equals

$$\Delta Y = \Delta I \times \text{Multiplier}$$

$$= \Delta I \times \frac{1}{1 - MPC}$$

Working of Multiplier

The working of the multiplier is based on the fact that one person's expenditure is another person's income.

Suppose we are given initial increase in investment is ₹ 900 Crore and MPC is .060.

Then multiplier (K) = $\frac{\Delta Y}{\Delta I}$ and total increase in income equals.

$$\Delta Y = \Delta I \times \text{Multiplier}$$

$$= 900 \times \frac{1}{1\text{-}0.60} = 900 \times \frac{1}{0.40}$$

= ₹ 2250 crore

Working of Investment Multiplier

(Δ I = 900, MPC = 0.60)

Round	ΔI (Increase in Investment)	ΔY (Increase in Income)	ΔC (Increase in consumption Expenditure)	ΔS (Increase in Savings)
I	900	900	540 (900x0.60)	360
II		540	324 (540x0.60)	216
III		324	194.40 (324x0.60)	129.60
IV		194.4	116.64 (194.4x0.60)	77.76
All Rounds		**₹2250**	**₹1350 = (2250x0.6)**	**₹900 = (2250x0.4)**

- Suppose an additional investment of ₹ 900 Crores (Δ I) is made to generate an extra income of ₹ 900 crore in first round. since MPC is 0.60, then recipients of this additional income will spend 60 percent of ₹ 900 crore i.e . ₹ 540 crore as consumption expenditure and remaining amount will be saved i.e. ₹ 560 crore. It will increase the income by ₹ 540 crore in round II.
- In the second round, 60 percent of additional income of ₹ 540 crore i.e. ₹ 324 crore will be spent on the consumption and remaining will be saved i.e. ₹ 216 crores.
- The multiplier process will go on till initial increase in investment by ₹ 900 crore leads to increase in income by ₹ 2250 crore. Income stops rising where initial increase in investment (Δ I) i.e. ₹ 900 crore becomes equal to increase in Saving (ΔS) i.e. ₹ 900 crore.

NUMERICAL ON MULTIPLIER AND EQUILIBRIUM

Problem–I:

Saving functions of an economy is S = –200 + .25Y

Economy is in equilibrium, when income is equal to 2000 calculate

(a) Investment expenditure of equilibrium level of income.

(b) Autonomous consumption.

(c) Investment multiplier.

Solution:

(a) S = – 200 + 0.25Y

= – 200 + 0.25 x 2000

(Equilibrium level of income (Y) = 200)

= ₹ 300

Since at equilibriums

Planned Savings (S) = Planned Investment (I)

∴ Investment Expenditure = ₹ 300

(b) (Income) Y = Consumption (C) + Saving (S)

When Y = 0 Savings are – 200

So Autonomous Consumption =₹200

(c) Investment multiplier (K) $= \frac{1}{\text{MPS}}$

$$K = \frac{1}{0.25} = 4.$$

Problem – II:

As a result of increase in investment, national income rises by ₹ 600 crores. If marginal propensity to consume is 0.75. Calculate increase in investment.

Solution:

$$\text{Multiplier (K)} = \frac{1}{\text{1-MPC}} = \frac{1}{1\text{-}0.75} = 4.$$

$$K = \frac{\Delta Y \text{ (Change in Income)}}{\Delta I \text{ (Change in Investment)}}$$

$$Y = \frac{600}{\Delta I}$$

$$\boxed{\therefore \Delta I = ₹\text{` } 150 \text{ crores}}$$

Problem–III:

Given consumption function C = 100 + 0.75Y and investment expenditure ₹ 1000. Calculate

(a) Equilibrium level of natural income.

(b) Consumption expenditure at equilibrium level of national income.

Solution:

(a) At equilibrium Y = C + I

$$= (100 + 0.75Y) + 1000$$

$$= ₹\ 4400$$

(b) Consumption expenditure of equilibrium level of income

$$C = 100 + .75Y$$

$$= 100 + .75 \times 4400$$

$$= ₹\ 3400$$

Formulae At A Glance

1. $$K = \frac{\Delta Y \text{ (Change in Income)}}{\Delta I \text{ (Change in Investment)}}$$

2. $$K = \frac{1}{1\text{-MPC}}, \; K = \frac{1}{\text{MPS}}$$

3. $$C = \overleftarrow{C} + bY$$

4. $$S = -\overleftarrow{C} + (1-b)\,Y$$

5. At equilibrium level of income

$$\frac{AD}{(C+Y)} = \frac{AS}{(C+S)} = Y$$

$$\boxed{\therefore Y = C + I}$$

Board Questions

Q. 1 **Discuss the working of adjustment mechanism in the following situation.**

(a) Aggregate demand is greater than aggregate supply.

(b) Ex ante Investment are lesser than Ex ante Savings. (CBSE 2019).

Q. 2 **Assume that increase in investment is ₹ 900 crore and marginal propensity to consume is 0.6. Explain the working of multiplier (CBSE 2017).**

Q. 3 **Given consumption curve, derive saving curve and state the steps of its derivation. Use diagram. (CBSE 2016, 2014).**

OR

Explain national income equilibrium through aggregate demand and aggregate supply. Use diagram. Also explain the change that takes place in an economy when the economy is not in equilibrium. (CBSE 2014).

Q. 4 C = 100 + 0.4 Y is the consumption function. Investment expenditure is 1100. Calculate

(a) Equilibrium level of national income.

(b) Consumption expenditure at equilibrium level of national income.

Hint: (1) Y = C+I

= 100+0.4Y+1100

=₹ 3000

(2) C = 100+0.4Y

= 100+0.4 x 3000

= ₹1300

3. 3 EXCESS DEMAND AND DEFICIENT DEMAND

ONE MARK QUESTIONS

Q. 1 Define excess demand.

Ans.: When in an economy, aggregate demand exceeds aggregate supply at full employment level, the demand is said to be excess demand.

Q. 2 Define deficient demand.

Ans.: When in an economy, aggregate demand is less than aggregate supply at full employment level of output it is called deficient demand.

Q. 3 What is inflationary gap?

Ans.: The gap which shows excess of AD over AS at full employment level is called inflationary gap.

Q. 4 What is deflationary gap?

Ans.: The gap which shows excess of AS over AD at the full employment level is called deflationary gap.

Q. 5 When will the situation of excess demand arise in the economy?

Ans.: When equilibrium level of income takes place after the stage of full employment it is a situation of excess demand.

Q. 6 **When will the situation of deficient demand arise in an economy?**

Ans.: When equilibrium level of income takes place before the stage of full employment it is a situation of deficient demand.

Q. 7 **What indicates under employment equilibrium?**

Ans.: Deficient demand indicates under employment equilibrium.

Q. 8 **What indicates over full employment equilibrium?**

Ans.: Excess demand indicates over full employment equilibrium.

Q. 9 **What is the impact of excess demand on the price level?**

Ans.: Excess demand bring inflation in the economy.

Q. 10 **What is the impact of deficient demand on the price level?**

Ans.: Deficient demand brings deflation in the economy.

Q. 11 **How does excess demand affect output and employment?**

Ans.: Output and employment remain unchanged as the equilibrium takes place after the stage of full employment.

Q. 12 **How does deficient demand affect output and employment?**

Ans.: Output and employment will decrease due to attainment of equilibrium before the full employment level.

Q. 13 **State the measures to correct excess demand and deficient demand.**

Ans.: The measures are:

(i) Fiscal measures

(ii) Monetary measures

Q. 14 **Define fiscal measures or fiscal policy measures.**

Ans.: It refers to taxation and expenditure decisions of the government to achieve economic objectives.

Q. 15 **Define monetary policy measures.**

Ans.: It is the power exercised by the central bank to influence money supply to achieve economic objectives.

Q. 16 **State the fiscal policy measure to correct excess demand.**

Ans.: The fiscal policy measures to correct excess demand are:

(i) Decrease in government spending.

(ii) Increase in taxes.

Q. 17 **State the fiscal policy measures to correct deficient demand.**

Ans.: The fiscal policy measures to correct deficient demand are:

(i) Increase in government spending.

(ii) Reduction in the taxes.

Q. 18 State the two measures of money supply.

Ans.: The two measures of money supply are:

(i) Quantitative method.

(ii) Qualitative method

Q. 19 What are quantitative instruments?

Ans.: Quantitative instruments include open market operations, CRR, SLR, reporate, reverse repo rate.

Q. 20 What are qualitative methods?

Ans.: Qualitative methods include margin requirements and moral suasion.

Q. 21 State the monetary policy measures to current excess demand and deficient demand.

Ans.:

Monetary Policy Measures

To Correct Excess Demand	**To Correct Deficient Demand**
1. Increase Bank Rate	1. Decrease Bank Rate
2. Increase CRR	2. Decrease CRR
3. Increase SLR	3. Decrease SLR
4. Increase Repo Rate	4. Decrease Repo Rate
5. Increase Reverse Repo Rate	5. Decrease Reverse Repo Rate
6. Sell Securities	6. Buy Securities
7. Raise Margin Requirements	7. Lower Margin Requirements

3–4 Marks Questions

Q. 1 Explain diagrammatically the situation of excess demand in an economy.

Ans.: When in an economy AD exceeds AS at full employment level, it is said to be excess demand and this gap is called inflationary gap.

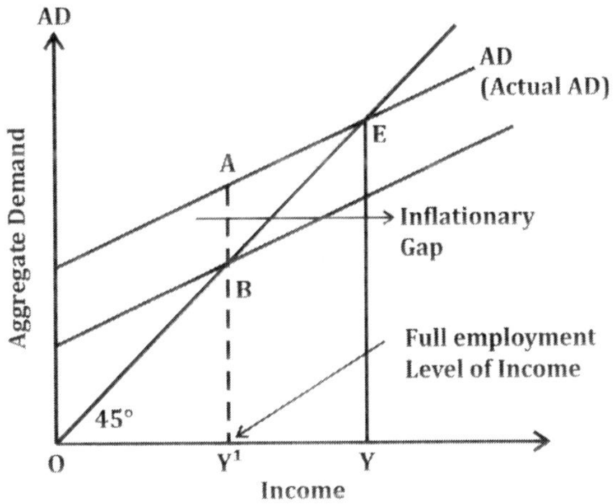

Explanation:

- Income is measured on X-axis and AD on Y-axis.
- E is the equilibrium point at the intersection of AD and 45° line i.e. over full employment equilibrium.
- AB is the inflationary gap at full employment level i.e. Y^1 where aggregate demand (AY^1) is greater than aggregate supply (BY^1).

Q. 2 How does excess demand bring in inflation?

Ans.: When AD is greater than AS, at full employment level, to overcome excess demand the producers overutilize the resources.

- As a result, price of inputs rises due to increase in demand for inputs.
- This led to rise in costs which compel the producers to raise the prices of the products which create inflation in the economy.

Q. 3 Explain diagrammatically the situation of deficient demand in an economy.

Ans.: When in an economy aggregate demand is less than aggregate supply at full employment level of output it is called deficient demand and this gap is called deflationary gap.

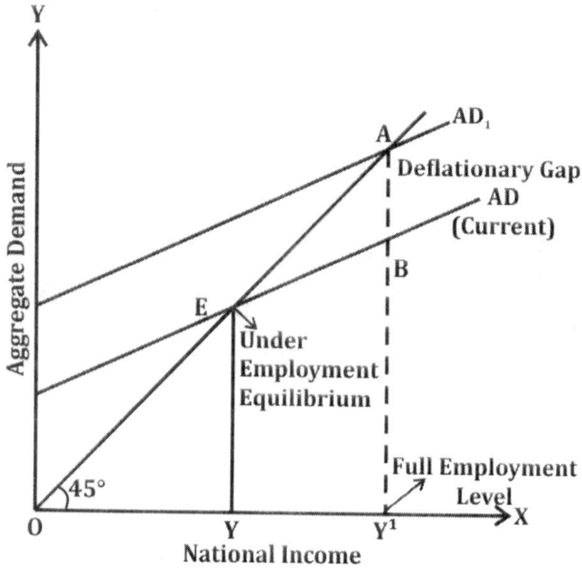

Explanation:

- Income is measured on X-axis and aggregate demand on Y^1-axis.
- E is the equilibrium point at the intersection of AD and 45° line i.e. under employment equilibrium.
- AB is the deflationary gap at full employment level i.e. (Y^1) where aggregate demand (AD) i.e. (BY^1) is less than aggregate supply (AY^1).

Q. 4 How does deficient demand bring deflation?

Ans.: When aggregate demand is less than aggregate supply at full employment level investment level is reduced.

- As a result, there is less demand for inputs than actually available.
- This leads to fall in the price of inputs.
- This creates deflationary situation in the economy.

Q. 5 Differentiate between inflationary gap and deflationary gap.

Ans.:

Inflationary Gap	*Deflationary Gap*
1. It is the gap of excess of AD over AS at full employment level.	It is gap of excess of AS over AD at full employment level.

(Contd...)

2. It is called situation of excess demand.	It is a situation of deficient demand.
3. It indicates over full employment equilibrium.	It indicates under employment equilibrium.
4. It leads to inflation.	It leads to deflation.
Reasons:	***Reasons:***
• Increase in household consumption demand	• Decrease in household consumption demand
• Increase in private investment demand due to rise in credit facilities.	• Decrease in private investment demand due to fall in credit facilities.
• Increase in government expenditure.	• Decrease in government expenditure.
• Increase in export demand.	• Decrease in export demand.

Q. 6 Explain fiscal measures to correct excess demand.

Ans.: The fiscal measures to correct excess demand are:

(1) Reducing Government Spending: Government reduces its various expenditure on education, defence, sanitation, welfare functions etc. which reduces aggregate demand in the economy and thus helps in removing inflationary gap.

(2) Increases Taxes: Increase in taxes reduces the disposable income of the people which in turn reduces their consumption expenditure. It reduces the aggregate demand in the economy and helpful in removing the inflationary gap.

Q. 7 Explain the fiscal measures to correct deficient demand in the economy.

Ans.: (1) Increase in spending by the Government. Government increases its various expenditure on various services like education, sanitation, defence, police, administration and welfare functions etc. This increases the aggregate demand in the economy which is helpful in removing deflationary gap.

(2) Reduces Taxes: Reduction in taxes increases the disposable income of the people which in turn increases their consumption expenditure. It will increase the aggregate demand in the economy and helpful in removing deflationary gap.

6 Marks Questions

Q. 1 Explain the monetary measures to correct excess demand and deficient demand.

Ans.: The various monetary policy measures are:

(1) Bank Rate

It is the interest rate at which the commercial banks can borrow from the central bank to meet their long-term needs.

During excess demand or inflation central bank raises it which increases the cost of borrowings for the commercial banks.

As a result, commercial banks raise their lending rates which discourages borrowers from taking loans and thus it reduces the aggregate demand in the economy.

During deficient demand or deflationary situation central bank lowers the bank rate which decreases the cost of borrowings for various banks.

As a result, the commercial banks lower their lending rates to encourage borrowings for investment purposes.

Thus, it increases the aggregate demand in the economy.

(2) CRR (Cash Reserve Rate)

It is the ratio of deposits which commercial banks have to keep with central bank as reserves.

During excess demand, central bank increases CRR to reduce excess reserves of commercial banks and thus reducing their lending capacity.

Borrowings from bank fall and as a result it reduces the aggregate demand.

During deficient demand, it decreases CRR to increase the funds available for credit creation.

Increase in credit creation capacity of the commercial banks leads to rise in borrowings and as a result AD rises.

(3) SLR (Statutory Liquidity Ratio)

It is the ratio of deposits which the commercial banks have to keep with themselves as reserves.

During excess demand, central bank increases SLR to reduce excess reserves of commercial banks and thus reducing their credit creation capacity. Borrowing from banks fall and as a result it reduces the AD.

During deficient demand, it decreases SLR to increase the funds available for credit creation.

Increase in credit creation capacity of the commercial banks leads to rise in borrowings and as a result AD rises.

(4) Repo Rate

It is the interest rate at which the commercial banks can borrow from the central bank to meet their short-term needs.

During excess demand, central bank raises it, which increases the cost of borrowings for the commercial banks.

As a result, commercial banks raises their lending rates which discourages borrowers from taking loans and thus it reduces the AD in the economy.

During deficient demand, central bank lowers it, which decreases the cost of borrowings for the commercial banks.

As a result, commercial banks lower their lending rates to encourage borrowings for investment purpose and thus AD rises.

(5) Reverse Repo Rate (RRR)

It is the interest rate at which the commercial banks can deposit their funds with the central bank.

During excess demand, central bank raises it which induces banks to transfer more funds to central bank due to attractive interest rates.

This reduces the liquidity with the commercial banks and effect their lending capacity.

Borrowings from banks be fall and as a result AD falls.

During deficient demand, central bank lower it which induces the commercial banks not to transfer more funds to central bank.

This increases the liquidity with them and raises their credit creation capacity.

Borrowings from banks rises, and as a result AD rises.

(6) Open Market Operations

It refers to buying and selling of securities by the central bank in the open market.

During excess demand, it starts selling securities to the open market.

It reduces the cash reserves of the commercial banks.

This in turn reduces the credits creation capacity of the commercial banks.

As a result, borrowings will fall and as a result AD falls.

During deficient demand, central bank purchases securities from the open market.

It increases the cash reserves of the commercial banks.

This in turn increase the credit creation capacity of the commercial banks.

As a result, borrowings rise, and as a result AD rises.

(7) Margin Requirements

It is a discount fixed by the central bank on the security mortgaged by the borrower to the commercial banks.

For Example: If a borrower mortgaged an asset worth ₹ 10 lakh, margin fixed is 20 percent by the central bank, then the commercial banks will be able to lend only 80 percent i.e. ₹ 8 lakh.

During excess demand, central bank raises it which discourages the borrowing capacity of public.

As a result, borrowings fall and AD fall.

During deficient demand, central bank lowers it. A fall in margin requirement encourages the people to borrow more.

As a result, borrowings rise and AD rises.

BOARD QUESTIONS

Q. 1 In the given figure, what does the gap 'KT' represent. State any two fiscal measures to correct the situation. (CBSE 2019).

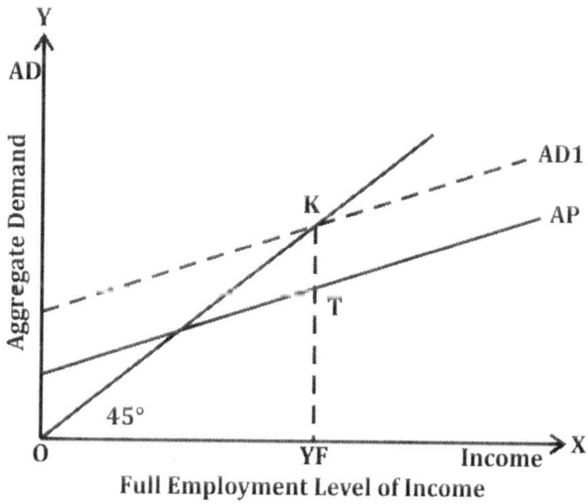

Q. 2 What is meant by inflationary gap? State three measures to reduce this gap. (CBSE 2018).

Q. 3 Explain the concept of deflationary gap and role of 'open market operations in reducing this gap'. (CBSE 2015).

OR

Explain concept of inflationary gap. Explain the role of repo rate in reducing this gap. (CBSE 2015).

Q. 4 Explain the concept of 'excess demand' in macroeconomics. Explain the role of open market operations in correcting it. (CBSE 2012).

UNIT–IV

Government Budget and the Economy

4.1 Government Budget

(i) Definition of government budget.

(ii) Objectives

(iii) Components

(iv) Budgeted Receipt: Revenue and Capital

(v) Budgeted Expenditure: Revenue and Capital

4.2 Deficits

(i) Primary deficit and its implications.

(ii) Fiscal deficit and its implications.

(iii) Revenue deficit and its implications.

4.1 GOVERNMENT BUDGET

Meaning, Objectives, Components

One Mark Questions

Q. 1 Define Government Budget.

Ans.: A government budget is an annual financial statement showing item wise estimates of expected revenue and anticipated expenditure during a fiscal year.

Q. 2 State the objectives of government Budget.

Ans.: The various objectives are:

(i) Allocation function (Influencing allocation of resources).

(ii) Redistribution of income (Reducing inequalities of income and wealth).

(iii) Stabilization function (Bringing economic stability).

Q. 3 State the components of budget.

Ans.: Two components of budget are:

(i) Budget receipts

(ii) Budget expenditure

Q. 4 Define Budget Receipts.

Ans.: It refers to the estimated money receipts of the government from various sources.

Q. 5 Define Budget Expenditure.

Ans.: It refers to the estimated expenditure of the government under various heads.

Q. 6 Name the Categories of Budget Receipt.

Ans.:

Categories of Budget Receipts

- Revenue Receipts
- Capital Receipts

Q. 7 Define Revenue Receipts.

Ans.: Revenue receipts are those receipts which neither create any liability nor cause any reduction in the assets of the government.

Q. 8 State the sources of revenue receipts.

Ans.: The Sources of Revenue Receipts

- Tax Revenue Receipts
- Non Tax Revenue Receipts

Q. 9 Define Tax Revenue.

Ans.: It refers to receipts from taxes and other duties imposed by the government.

Q. 10 Define Tax.

Ans.: Tax is a legally compulsory payment made by the people to the government.

Q. 11 Define Direct Tax.

Ans.: When liability to pay a tax and burden of it falls on the same person, it is called direct tax.

For Example: Income tax, corporation tax (tax on income of companies), wealth tax etc.

Q. 12 Define Indirect Tax.

Ans.: When liability to pay a tax and its burden falls on the other person, it is called indirect tax.

For Example: Goods and Service Tax.

Q. 13 Define Non-Tax Revenue.

Ans.: It refers to income receipts from all sources other than the tax.

Q. 14 State the sources of Non-Tax Revenue.

Ans.: The various sources of Non-Tax Revenue are:

(1) Dividends

(2) Interest

(3) profits

(4) External Grants

(5) Fines and Penalties

(6) License Fees, Other Fees (Court Fees, Registration Fees etc.).

Q. 15 Define Capital Receipts.

Ans.: Capital receipts are those receipts which, either create liabilities or reduce the assets of the government.

Q. 16 State the sources of Capital Receipts.

Ans.: The sources of Capital Receipts are:

(1) Borrowings and other liabilities.

(2) Recovery of loans.

(3) Other capital receipts.

Q. 17 What are the categories of budget expenditure?

Ans.:

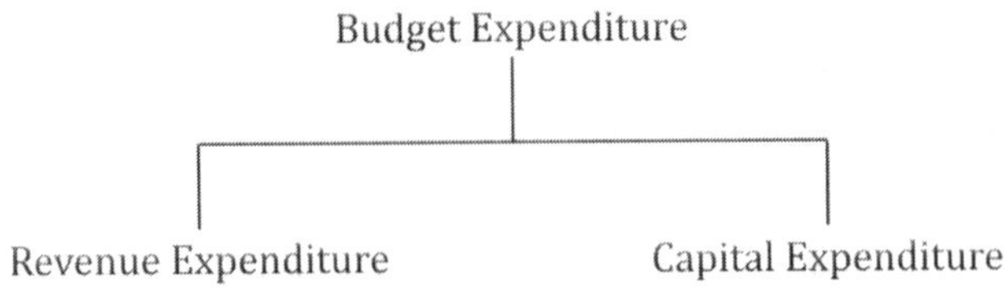

Q. 18 Define Revenue Expenditure.

Ans.: It refers to the expenditure which does not lead to any creation of assets or reduction in liabilities.

For Example: Salary, Pension, Grants etc.

Q. 19 Define Capital Expenditure.

Ans.: It refers to the expenditure which leads to creation of assets or reduction in liabilities.

For Example: Purchase of shares, Expenditure on land, building etc.

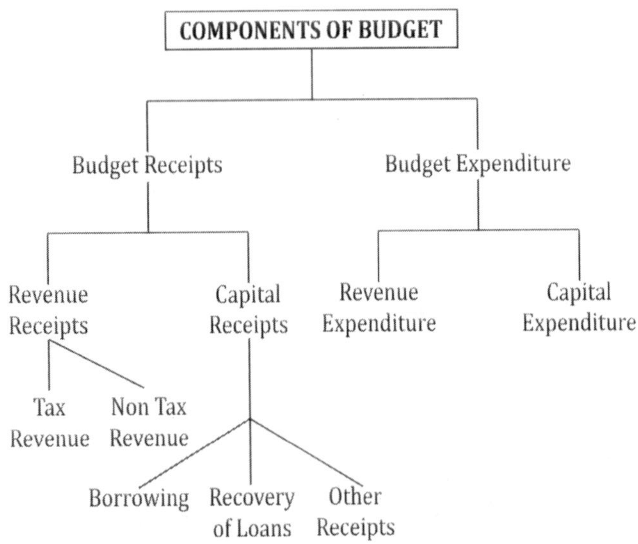

3–4 Marks Questions

Q. 1 Explain 'Allocation Function' as an objective of government budget.

Ans.:

- Private sectors always undertake those economic activities where profits are high. It is not interested to allocate resources to those areas of production where huge expenditure is involved.
- Through its budgetary policy, government aims to reallocate resources in such a manner that there is a balance between the goal of profit maximization and social welfare.
- Production of goods which are injurious to health (like liquor, cigarettes etc.) is discouraged through heavy taxation.
- Production of socially useful goods (like khadi products) is encouraged through subsidies.
- By doing so, government helps in influencing allocation of resources.

Q. 2 Explain 'Stabilization function' as an objective.

Ans.:

- Absence of large-scale fluctuation in price level is called economic stability.
- It leads to more investment and increases the rate of growth and development.
- Government expenditure and taxes helps to control these fluctuations in inflation and deflation.
- Governments reduce its own expenditure and discourage spending by increasing taxes during inflation.
- Governments increase its own expenditure in the interest of the people and encourage spending by giving subsidies at the time of deflation.
- This it achieves its stabilization function.

Q. 3 Explain 'Redistribution of Income' as an objective of the government.

Ans.:

- Government uses fiscal instruments of taxation and subsidies to achieve this objective.
- Government can impose higher rates of taxes on income of rich people.

- Similarly, it gives subsidies to the poor section or spending more on the welfare of the people like free education, medical aid etc.
- In this way, it will reduce disposable income of the rich and raises standard of living of the poor.
- Thus, gap between rich and poor can be reduced and is helpful in reducing income inequalities in the country.

Q. 4 Explain the sources of Non-Tax Revenues.

Ans.: The sources of Non-Tax Revenues are:

I. COMMERCIAL REVENUE

(1) Interest received on loans given to state government, private enterprises.

(2) Dividend on investments made by the government.

(3) Profits through public sector undertakings like Indian Railways, LIC etc.

II. ADMINISTRATIVE REVENUE

(1) Fees: Payment made to the government for rendering services to us.

(2) License Fees: It is payment made to the government on granting permission for something.

For Example: Driving License.

(3) Fines: Payment which are imposed on breaking the rules of the government.

For Example: Jumping a red light, not wearing a helmet etc.

Q. 5 Differentiate between Direct Tax and Indirect Tax.

Ans.:

DIRECT TAX	*INDIRECT TAX*
1. When liability to pay a tax and burden of it falls on the same person it is called Direct Tax.	When liability to pay a tax and the burden falls on the other person it is called Indirect Tax.
2. It is progressive in nature i.e. tax rate increases with the increase in income and vice versa. *For Example:* Income Tax, corporation Tax, Wealth Tax.	It is proportional in nature as burden of tax is more on poor than rich. *For Example:* Goods and Service Tax (GST).

Q. 6 Explain the sources of 'Capital Receipts'.

Ans.: The sources of Capital Receipts are:

(1) Borrowings and Other Liabilities: These are capital receipts as they create a liability for the government. This is because government borrows from central bank (RBI), foreign governments, open market, to meet its excess expenditure.

(2) Recovery of Loans: It reduces the assets of the government at the time of recovering loans from the debtors against their assets. Government grants various types of loans to state government, etc.

(3) Other Capital Receipts: Government held share of the public sector enterprises. when government acquires funds by selling its equity holdings it is called disinvestment. It leads to reduction in the assets held by the government.

Q. 7 Distinguish between Capital Receipts and Revenue Receipts.

Ans.:

CAPITAL RECEIPTS	*REVENUE RECEIPTS*
1. Receipts which either create liabilities or reduce the assets of the government are called capital receipts.	The receipts which neither create any liabilities nor cause any reduction in assets of the government are called revenue receipts.
2. These are irregular in nature	These are regular in nature.
3. It creates further obligation to return the amount.	It does not create further obligation.
4. Three sources – Other Receipts, Borrowings, Recovery of Loans.	Two Sources – Tax and Non-Tax sources.

Q. Distinguish between Revenue Expenditure and Capital Expenditure.

Ans.:

REVENUE EXPENDITURE	*CAPITAL EXPENDITURE*
1. It is the expenditure which does not lead to any creation of assets or reduction in liabilities.	It is the expenditure which leads to creation of assets or reduction in liabilities.
2. These are regular in nature.	These are irregular.
3. It is also called non developmental expenditure. *For Example:* Salary, Pension, Interest, Grants etc.	It is also called developmental expenditure. *For Example:* Expenditure on Land, Building, Giving Loans etc.

BOARD QUESTIONS

Q. 1 **How are tax receipts different from non-tax receipts? State any two items of revenue expenditure in a government budget. (CBSE 2019).**

Q. 2 **Explain the following objectives:**

(1) Allocation of resources.

(2) Reducing income inequalities. (CBSE 2018)

Q. 3 **Explain the basis of classifying taxes into direct and indirect tax. Give examples. (CBSE 2017).**

Q. 4 **Explain how government budget can be used to influence distribution of income. (CBSE 2017).**

Q. 5 **What is government budget? Explain how taxes and subsidies can be used to influence allocation of resources. (CBSE 2016).**

Q. 6 **Explain the role of the government can play through the budget in influencing allocation of resources (CBSE 2015, 2011).**

Q. 7 **Tax rates on higher income group have been increased. Which economic value does it reflect? Classify into capital and revenue receipts. (CBSE 2014).**

(1) Tax receipts

(2) Disinvestment

Q. 8 **Distinguish between revenue and capital expenditure. Give an example of each. CBSE 2013).**

4.2 DEFICITS

ONE MARK QUESTIONS

Q. 1 **Define Government Deficit.**

Ans.: It is defined as excess of total estimated expenditure over total estimated revenue.

Q. 2 **What are the types of government deficits?**

Ans.: The types of government deficits are:

(1) Revenue Deficit

(2) Fiscal Deficit

(3) Primary Deficit

Q. 3 Define Revenue Deficit.

Ans.: It refers to excess of total revenue expenditure over total revenue receipts.

$$\text{Revenue Deficit} = \text{Total Revenue Expenditure} - \text{Total Revenue Receipts}$$

Q. 4 Define Fiscal Deficit.

Ans.: It refers to excess of total expenditure over total receipts (excluding borrowing) during the given fiscal year.

(1) $\text{Fiscal Deficit} = \text{Total Expenditure} - \text{Total Receipts excluding Borrowings}$

(2) When only total borrowings are given

Fiscal Deficit = Borrowing

Q. 5 Define Primary Deficit.

Ans.: It is difference between fiscal deficit and interest Payment.

Primary Deficit = Fiscal Deficit – Interest Payments

Q. 6 What are Non-Debt Creating Capital Receipts?

Ans.: It includes all the capital receipts excluding borrowings.

Q. 7 State the measures to Reduce Revenue Deficit.

Ans.: **Measures to Reduce Revenue Deficit**

Reduce Expenditure

Government should avoid unproductive or unnecessary expenditure.

Increase Revenue

Government should increase its receipts from various sources of tax and non-tax revenues.

Q. 8 State the measures to Reduce Fiscal Deficit.

Ans.: **Measures to Reduce Fiscal Deficit**

Borrowing

It can be met through borrowing from internal and external sources.

Deficit Financing

RBI issues new currency when government borrow from RBI against its securities.

3–4 Marks Questions

Q. 1 What are the implications of fiscal deficit?

Ans.: The implications are:

(1) Inflation: To meet the fiscal deficit, government borrows from RBI. In increases the money supply in the economy as RBI prints new currency notes to cover this deficit. It leads to inflation due to increase in the money supply.

(2) Foreign Dependence: Government also has to borrow from other countries to meet excess expenditures.

(3) Debt Trap: Borrowing requirements of the government also include interest payments. It increases the revenue expenditure which create revenue deficit. So, to meet deficit, government take more loans to repay the earlier loans so the country has to face debt trap.

Q. 2 What are the implications of revenue deficit?

Ans.: The implications are:

(1) It signifies that government is unable to meet its revenue expenditure fully from its revenue receipts.

(2) It indicates dissaving on part of government.

(3) To cover this deficits government is forced to use sources of capital receipts. i.e. through borrowings or disinvestment.

(4) It leads to an inflationary situation as the government is using sources of capital receipts to meet extra consumption expenditure.

Q. 3 What are the implications of primary deficit?

Ans.: Implications of primary deficit:

(1) It indicates borrowing requirements of the government to meet excess expenditure other than interest payments.

(2) It indicates that government borrowings create more future problems.

(3) A low or zero primary deficits indicates that government is concerned with future problems.

(4) A high primary deficit indicates that government is not able to overcome future problems created by borrowings.

Q. 4 Differentiate between Fiscal Deficit and Revenue Deficit.

Ans.:

FISCAL DEFICIT	*REVENUE DEFICIT*
1. It refers to excess of total expenditure over total receipts excluding borrowings.	It refers to excess of revenue expenditure over revenue receipts.
2. It indicates the borrowing requirements of the government.	It indicates the inability of the government to meet its regular expenditure.

Q. 5 Distinguish between Fiscal Deficit and Primary Deficit.

Ans.:

FISCAL DEFICIT	*PRIMARY DEFICIT*
1. It refers to excess of total expenditure over total receipts excluding borrowings.	It refers to difference between fiscal deficit and interest payment.
2. It indicates the total borrowing requirements including interest of the government.	It indicates the total borrowing requirements excluding interest of the government.
3. Fiscal Deficit = Total Expenditure – Total receipts excluding borrowings.	Primary deficit = Fiscal deficit – Interest Payments.

Numericals

Problem–1:

From the following find out Revenue Deficit, Fiscal Deficit, Primary Deficit.

	(₹ Arab)
(i) Capital receipts net of borrowing	95
(ii) Revenue Expenditure	100
(iii) Interest Payments	10
(iv) Revenue Receipts	80
(v) Capital Expenditure	110

Solution:

(a) Revenue Deficit = ii – iv

= 100 – 80 = ₹ 20 Arab

(b) Fiscal Deficit = (ii + v) – iv – i

= (100 + 110) – 80 – 95 = ₹ 35 Arab

(c) Primary Deficit = Fiscal Deficit – iii

= 35 – 10 = ₹ 25 Arab

Problem – 2

In a government budget, revenue deficit is ₹ 50,000 Crore and borrowings are ₹ 75,000 Crore. Calculate Fiscal Deficit.

Sollution:

Fiscal Deficit = ₹ 75,000 Crores

(As Fiscal Deficit is equal to the borrowings).

Board Questions

Q. 1 **What is meant by primary deficit or fiscal deficit? (CBSE 2019, 2017)**

Q. 2 **Give the meaning of revenue deficit, fiscal deficit, primary deficit. (CBSE 2018).**

Q. 3 **Distinguish between revenue deficit and fiscal deficit. (CBSE 2013).**

Q. 4 **Explain revenue deficit. What does it indicate? (CBSE 2012).**

Unit – V

Balance of Payments

5.1 Exchange Rate

(i) Meaning

(ii) Types of exchange rates.

(iii) Sources of demand and supply of foreign exchange.

(iv) Concept of appreciation, depreciation, revaluation and devaluation of domestic currency.

(v) Determination of flexible exchange rate.

5.2 Balance of Payments

(i) Meaning

(ii) Components of Balance of Payment Account.

(iii) Components of Current Account and Capital Account.

(iv) Autonomous and Accommodation Transactions.

(v) Meaning of Balance of Payments Deficit.

5.1 EXCHANGE RATE

One Mark Questions

Q. 1 Define Foreign Exchange.

Ans.: It refers to all currencies other than the domestic currency of a given country.

Q. 2 Define Exchange Rate.

Ans.: It is the rate at which one currency can be converted or exchanged into another currency.

For Example: One US dollar can be obtained by paying ₹ 70. Then the exchange rate is 1 US Dollar = ₹ 70.

Q. 3 What are the types of Exchange Rate?

Ans.: The types of Exchange Rate are:

(1) Fixed Exchange Rate

(2) Flexible Exchange Rate or Floating Exchange Rate.

(3) Managed Floating Rate or Dirty Floating Rate.

Q. 4 Define Fixed Exchange Rate.

Ans.: It is the rate that is fixed and determined by the government of country.

Q. 5 Define Flexible Exchange Rate.

Ans.: It is the rate which is determined by the demand for and supply of different currencies in the foreign exchange market.

Q. 6 Define Managed Floating Rate.

Ans.: It is the rate which is floating and is influenced by the intervention of the central bank in the foreign exchange market.

Q. 7 State the purpose of central bank in influencing floating rate.

Ans.: Central bank attempts to influence their countries exchange rate by buying and selling currencies to maintain a certain range. This is done for the interest of importers and exporters.

Q. 8 What is Currency Depreciation?

Ans.: Depreciation of domestic currency means a fall in the price of domestic currency in terms of foreign currency in the foreign exchange market.

Q. 9 What is Currency Appreciation?

Ans.: Appreciation of domestic currency means a rise in the price of domestic currency in terms of foreign currency in the foreign exchange market.

Q. 10 What is devaluation of domestic currency?

Ans.: It refers to official lowering of the value of domestic currency against foreign currency by the government.

Q. 11 What is revaluation of domestic currency?

Ans.: It refers to official raising of the value of domestic currency against foreign currency by the government.

Q. 12 What is the shape of demand curve of foreign exchange?

Ans.: Demand curve of foreign exchange slopes downward due to inverse relationship between demand for foreign exchange and foreign exchange rate.

Q. 13 What is the shape of supply curve of foreign exchange?

Ans.: Supply curve of foreign exchange slopes upward due to direct relationship between supply for foreign exchange and foreign exchange rate.

Q. 14 What leads to change in exchange rate?

Ans.: Exchange rate changes due to:

(1) Change in demand (Increase and decrease).

(2) Change in supply (Increase and decrease).

Q. 15 How can RBI help in bringing down the foreign exchange rate which is very high?

Ans.: RBI can increase the supply of foreign exchange by selling foreign exchange from its reserves to bring down its value.

3–4 Marks Questions

Q. 1 Explain the effect of currency depreciation on exports.

Ans.: The currency is said to be depreciated when there is decrease in the value of domestic currency in terms of foreign currency.

It means that a country has to pay more units of domestic currency to obtain one unit of foreign currency.

For Example: If price of one US dollar rises from ₹ 60 to ₹ 65, the Indian Rupee is said to be depreciated.

Effect on Exports:

- Export will increase due to depreciation of domestic currency.
- This is due to the reason that goods become cheaper for foreign countries and more goods can be purchased from domestic country (India) with same amount of Dollars.

Q. 2 Explain the effect of currency appreciation on imports.

Ans.: The currency is said to be appreciated when there is increase in the value of domestic currency in terms of foreign currency.

It means that a country has to pay less units of domestic currency to obtain one unit of foreign currency.

For Example: If the price of one dollar falls from ₹‘ 65 to ₹ 60, the Indian Rupee is said to be appreciated.

Effect on Imports:

Imports will increase due to appreciation of domestic currency.

This is due to the reason that goods become cheaper for domestic country (India).

So, more goods can be purchased from foreign countries (U.S.A.) with the same amount of money.

Q. 3 Distinguish between devaluation and depreciation of domestic currency.

Ans.:

DEVALUATION	*DEPRECIATION*
1. It refers to official lowering of the value of domestic currency against foreign currency by the government.	It refers to fall in the price of domestic currency in terms of foreign currency in the foreign exchange market.
2. It takes place under fixed exchange rate.	It takes place under flexible exchange rate.
3. It is determined by the monetary authority of the country.	It is determined by market forces of demand and supply.

Q. 4 Distinguish between Revaluation and Appreciation

Ans.:

REVALUATION	*APPRECIATION*
1. It refers to official raising of the value of domestic currency against foreign currency by the government.	It refers to rise in the price of domestic currency in term of foreign currency in the foreign exchange market.
2. It takes place under fixed exchange rate.	It takes place under flexible exchange rate.
3. It is determined by the monetary authority of the country.	It is determined by market forces of demand and supply.

Q. 5 Distinguish between Depreciation and Appreciation.

Ans.:

DEPRECIATION	*APPRECIATION*
1. It refers to fall in the price of domestic currency in terms of foreign currency in the foreign exchange market.	It refers to rise in the price of domestic currency in terms of foreign currency in the foreign exchange market.
2. It leads in increase in exports. *For Example:* If price of one US Dollar rises from ₹ 60 to ₹ 65, Indian Rupee is said to be depreciated.	It leads to increase in imports. *For Example:* If price one US dollar falls from ₹ 65 to ₹` 60, the Indian Rupee is said to be appreciated.

Q. 6 Explain the relation between Foreign Exchange Rate and Demand for It.

OR

Why demand curve of foreign exchange is downward sloping?

OR

When price of foreign currency rises, its demand falls. Explain why?

Ans.: Demand curve of foreign exchange slopes downwards due to inverse relationship between demand for foreign exchange and foreign exchange rate.

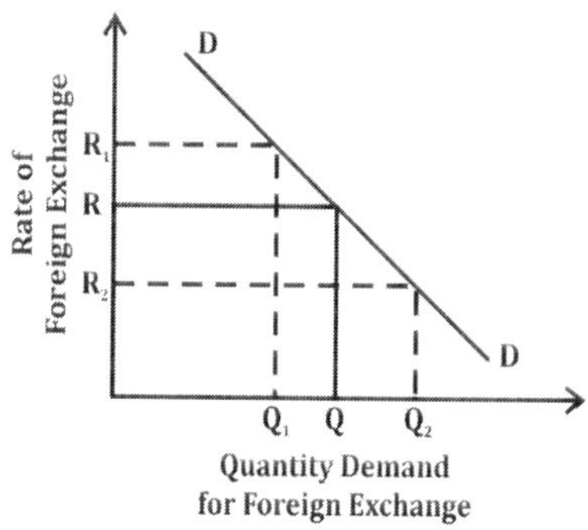

- If price of foreign exchange falls from OR to OR_2, more of foreign currency is demanded to purchase foreign goods and services. As a result, imports increase and demand for foreign exchange rises.
- If price of foreign exchange rises from OR to OR_1, less of foreign currency is demanded. This results in fall in the demand for foreign goods and services by the domestic residents.
- As a result, imports decline. As a result, demand for foreign exchange falls.

Q. 7 Explain the relation between foreign exchange rate and supply for it?

OR

Why supply curve of foreign exchange is upward sloping.

OR

When price of foreign currency rises, its supply also rises. Explain why?

Ans.:

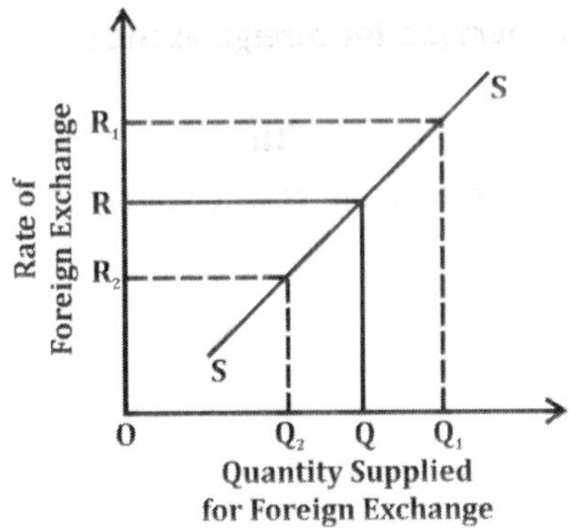

- Supply curve of foreign exchange slopes upward due to direct relationship between supply of foreign exchange and foreign exchange rate.
- If price of foreign exchange falls from OR to OR_2, supply of foreign currency is reduced. This is because domestic goods have become costlier for the foreign residents.
- If price of foreign exchange rises from OR to OR_1 supply of foreign currency is increased.
- This is because domestic goods have become cheaper for the foreign residents.
- This leads to an increase in the exports of domestic country as a result domestic country receives more foreign currency and its supply rises.

Q. 8 State the sources of demand of foreign exchange.

OR

Why people desire to have foreign exchange.

Ans.: The sources of demand of foreign exchange are:

(1) Tourism: Foreign exchange is demanded for foreign tours.

(2) Import of Goods and Services: It is demanded to make the payment for imports of goods and services.

(3) For making transfer payments in the form of gifts, donations, financial help to families etc.

(4) For purchasing an asset like land, shares etc. in the foreign countries.

(5) For lending money and for making repayments to foreign countries.

Q. 9 Why does demand for foreign exchange rises, when its price falls?

OR

What are the reasons of 'rise in demand' for foreign currency?

Ans.: The demand for foreign currency rises due to:

(1) When price of foreign currency falls, imports from that foreign country become cheaper so imports increases and demand for foreign currency rises.

(2) When price of foreign currency falls, it promotes tourism. As a result, demand for foreign currency rises.

(3) When price of foreign currency falls, people will like to purchases financial assets. As a result, demand for foreign currency rises.

(4) When price of foreign currency falls, people will like to make transfer payments in the form of gifts, donations etc. As a result, demand for foreign currency rises.

Q. 10 State reasons of supply of foreign exchange.

OR

State sources of supply of foreign exchange.

Ans.: The sources of supply are:

(1) Tourism: Supply of foreign exchange increases when foreigners visit our country.

(2) Supply of foreign exchange comes through exports of goods and service.

(3) Supply of foreign exchange increases in the form of transfer payments through donations, cash, remittances etc.

(4) Supply of foreign exchange comes when foreigners make investments (land etc.) in the domestic country.

(5) Supply of foreign exchange comes from borrowing money and receiving repayments from foreign countries.

Q. 11 Why does a rise in foreign exchange rate causes a rise in foreign exchange supply?

OR

What are the reasons of 'rise in supply' of foreign currency?

Ans.: The supply of foreign currency rises due to:

(1) When price of foreign currency rises, foreign direct investment increases, which will increase the supply of foreign exchange.

(2) When price of foreign currency rises, exports increases as domestic goods become relatively cheaper, so it increases the supply of foreign exchange.

(3) When price of foreign currency rises, foreigners will like to visit domestic country, so it increases the supply of foreign exchange.

(4) When price of foreign currency rises, supply of foreign exchange increases in the form of transfer payments through donations, cash remittances etc.

Q. 12 How is foreign exchange rate determined? Use diagram.

Ans.: Exchange rate is determined at the equilibrium point where demand for foreign exchange and supply of foreign exchange are equal.

- Demand Curve is downward sloping due to inverse relationship between demand for foreign exchange and foreign exchange rate.
- Supply curve is upward sloping due to direct relationship between supply for foreign exchange and foreign exchange rate.

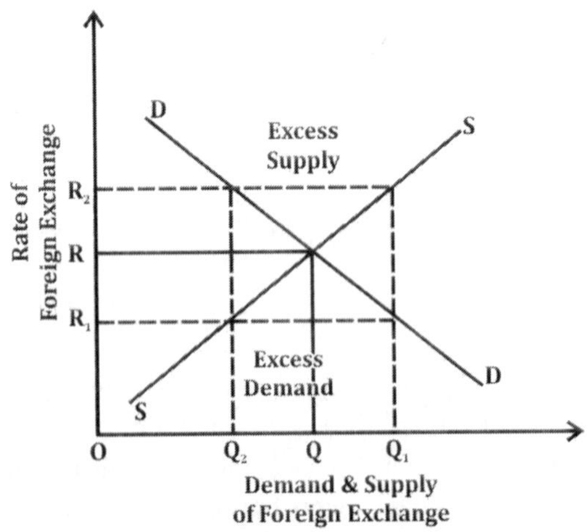

Explanations:

- DD is demand curve.
- SS is the supply curve.
- Both intersect at point E; equilibrium exchange rate is OR.
- If the exchange rate rises to OR_2, it is a situation of excess supply where demand falls to OQ_2 and supply rises to OQ_1.
- Due to excess supply, exchange rate will fall till it reaches the equilibrium level of OR.
- If the exchange rate falls to OR_1, it is a situation of excess demand where demand rises to OQ_1 and supply falls to OQ_2.
- Due to excess demand, the exchange rate will rise till it reaches the equilibrium level of OR.

Effect of Changes in Demand and Supply on Exchange Rate

INCREASE IN DEMAND

Increase in Demand

↓

Situation of Excess Demand

↓

Exchange Rate Rises

↓

Domestic Currency Depreciated

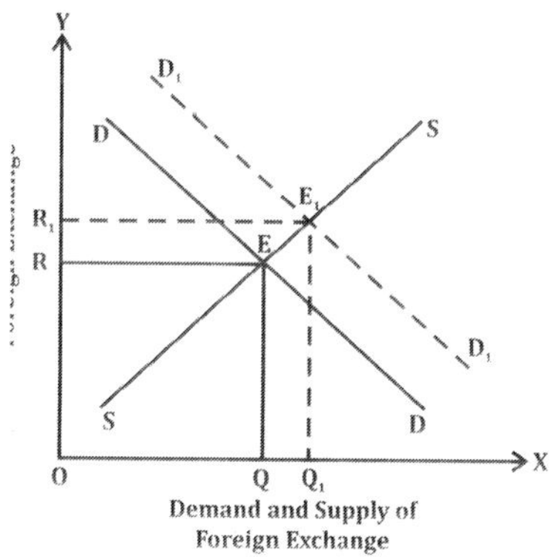

DECREASE IN SUPPLY

Decrease in Supply

↓

Situation of Deficit Supply

↓

Exchange Rate Rises

↓

Domestic Currency Depreciated

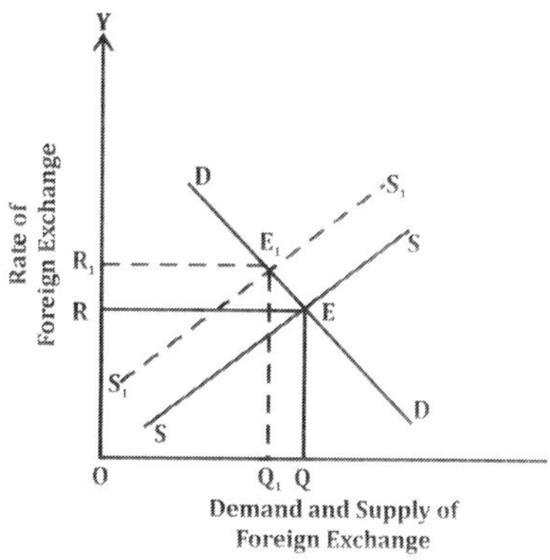

Ans.: Explanation:

- IDD is demand curve.
- SS is supply curve.
- Both intersect at point E which is the equilibrium.
- When demand increases from DD to D_1D_1 new equilibrium shift to E1 exchange rate increases to OR1.

Examples:

(1) Visit to foreign countries by the people of India.

(2) Imports of goods from China.

(3) Indian students going to foreign countries for higher studies.

(4) Purchase of an asset by an Indian in a foreign country.

Explanation:

- DD is the demand curve.
- SS is the supply curve.
- Both intersect at point E which is the equilibrium.
- When supply decreases from SS to S_1S_1 equilibrium shifts from E to E_1 and exchange rate increases to OR_1.

Examples:

(1) When foreign tourists do not like to visit domestic country.

(2) When foreigners do not like to invest in the home country.

DECREASE IN DEMAND

Decrease in Demand
↓
Deficit Demand
↓
Exchange Rate Falls
↓
Domestic Currency Appreciated

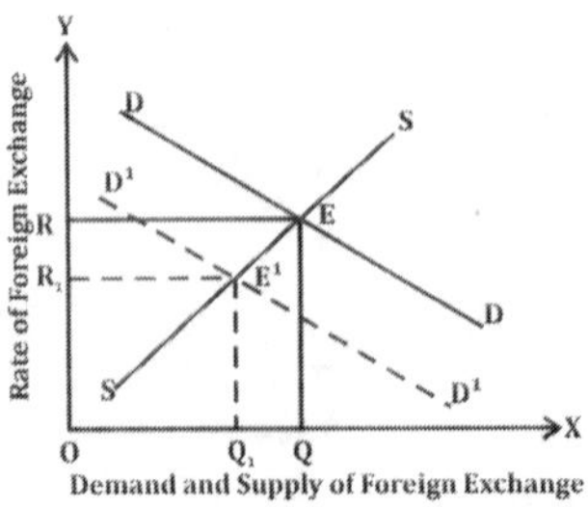

INCREASE IN SUPPLY

Increase in Supply
↓
Situation of Excess Supply
↓
Exchange Rate Falls
↓
Domestic Currency Appreciated

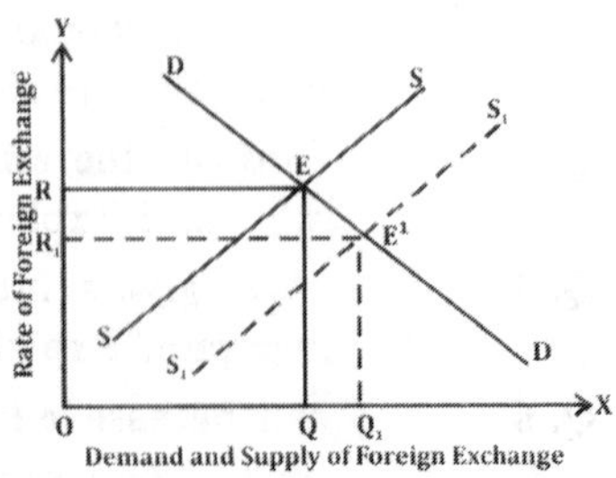

Ans.:

Explanation:	**Explanation:**
• DD and SS are demand and supply curves which intersect point E (equilibrium). • When demand decreases from DD to D_1D_1 new equilibrium shifts from E to E_1 and exchange rate falls to OR_1.	• DD and SS are demand and at supply curve which intersect at point E (equilibrium). • When supply increases from SS to S_1S_1 new equilibrium shifts from E to E_1 and exchange rate falls to OR_1.
Examples:	**Examples:**
• Government of India has doubled the import duty on gold.	• Foreigners visit India for sightseeing etc. Exports of goods to China. Purchase of land in India by a foreigner. Borrowings from abroad. Increase in foreign direct investment.

Board Questions

Q. 1 **"Indian Rupee (₹) plunged to all time low of ₹ 74.48 against the US dollar ($). (The Economic Times).**

In the light of above report, discuss the impact of the situation on Indian Rupee. (CBSE 2019).

Q. 2 **Explain the impact of rise in exchange rate on national income. (CBSE 2018).**

(Hint: National income is likely to rise as rise in exchange rate will increase the exports).

Q. 3 **Why does the demand for foreign currency fall and supply rises when its price rises? Explain. (CBSE 2017).**

Q. 4 **What will be the effect of foreign investment in India on exchange rate? Explain. (CBSE 2016).**

Q. 5 **How does giving incentives for exports influence foreign exchange rate? Explain. (CBSE 2014).**

Q. 6 **How can increase in foreign direct investment affect the price of foreign exchange? (CBSE 2013).**

Q. 7 **Define managed floating exchange rate. (CBSE 2012).**

Q. 8 **When price of foreign currency rises, its demand falls. Explain why? (CBSE 2011).**

Q. 9 **Distinguish between devaluation and depreciation of domestic currency. (CBSE 2010).**

5.2 BALANCE OF PAYMENTS

One Mark Questions

Q. 1 **Define balance of payments account.**

Ans.: It is an accounting statement showing systematic record of country's sources and uses of foreign exchange during a given period of time.

Q. 2 **State the sources of Balance of payments account.**

Ans.: The sources of foreign exchange are: Exports, Foreign Investment, Transfers from Abroad, Income from Investment Abroad etc.

Q. 3 **State the uses of balance of payments account.**

Ans.: The uses of foreign exchange are: Imports, Incomes paid on Foreign Investments, Transfers to Abroad, Investment Abroad etc.

Q. 4 **State the two sides of Balance of Payments Account.**

Ans.: The two sides of balance of payment account are:

(1) **Credit:** Inflows of Foreign Exchange.

(2) **Debit:** Outflows of Foreign Exchange.

Q. 5 **What are the two main components of Balance of Payments Account?**

Ans.: The main components are:

(1) Current Account

(2) Capital Account

Q. 6 **What is a current account?**

Ans.: Current account is an account which record all the transactions relating to country's sources and uses of foreign exchange on account of flow of goods and services, unilateral transfers and incomes from and to abroad.

Q. 7 **What are components of current account?**

Ans.: The components of current account are:

A. Visibles

Import and export of goods.

B. Invisibles

   (i) Services

   (ii) Transfers

   (iii) Incomes

Q. 8 What is a capital account?

Ans.: It is an account which record all the transactions relating to country's sources and uses of foreign exchange on account of transactions which causes changes in foreign financial assets and liabilities.

Q. 9 What are the components of capital account?

Ans.: The components of capital account are:

(1) Investments to and from abroad.

(2) Borrowings and lending.

(3) Official reserve transactions or change in foreign exchange reserves.

Q. 10 What is balance of trade or trade balance?

Ans.: It is the difference between amount of exports and imports goods.

Q. 11 What is trade surplus?

Ans.: When exports are greater than imports it is called trade surplus.

Q. 12 What is trade deficit?

Ans.: When exports are less than imports it called trade deficit.

Q. 13 What is the balance on current account?

Ans.: It is defined as the difference between the sum of credits and sum of debits on current account.

Q. 14 What is the balance on capital account?

Ans.: It is defined as the difference between the sum of credits and sum of debits on capital account.

Q. 15 What is an autonomous transaction?

Ans.: International economic transactions which takes place due to some economic motive like earning income or profit are called autonomous transactions.

Q. 16 What is an accommodating transaction?

Ans.: Transactions that are undertaken to cover deficit or surplus in autonomous transactions are called accommodating transactions.

Q. 17 What is deficit in balance of payment account?

Ans.: A deficit in balance of payment occurs when total inflows on account of autonomous transactions are less than total outflow on account of autonomous transactions.

Q. 18 What is surplus in balance of payment account?

Ans.: When autonomous inflow of foreign exchange exceeds autonomous outflow, it is called surplus in balance of payment account.

3–4 Marks Questions

Q. 1 Explain the components of current account.

Ans.: The components of current account are:

I. VISIBLES (merchandise): It implies import and export of goods.

- Payment for import of goods are recorded as debit because it leads to outflow of foreign exchange.
- Receipts from exports of goods are recorded as credit because it brings in foreign exchange.

II. INVISIBLES

A. **Services** like shipping, banking, tourism, transportation etc.

Payment for these services taken are recorded on debit side because it leads to outflow of foreign exchange.

Receipts from these services rendered are recorded on credit side because it brings in foreign exchange.

B. **Transfers** include gifts, personal remittances, donations etc. for which the provider does not get anything in return.

Payment of transfers to rest of the world is recorded on debit side.

Receipts of transfers recorded on credit side.

C. **Incomes:** It includes

(i) Investment Income which is in the form of interest, dividends, rent etc.

Investment earnings paid to non-resident is recorded on debit side.

Investment earnings received by the residents is recorded on credit side.

(ii) Compensation of employees.

Wages and salaries paid by residents is recorded on debit side.

Wages and salaries received by residents is recorded on credit side.

Q. 2 Explain the components of capital account.

Ans.: The components of capital account are:

I. Investments

Investments by Indian residents in shares of foreign companies, real estate etc. are recorded on debit side as they lead to outflow of foreign exchange.

Investments by rest of the world in shares of Indian companies, real estate etc. are recorded on credit side as they bring in foreign exchange.

II. Borrowing and Lending

Transactions of lending to abroad by private individuals, government and repayment of loans to abroad are recorded on debit side.

Transactions of borrowing from abroad by private sector, government and repayment of loans by foreigners are recorded on credit side.

III. Official Reserve Transactions

These are those transactions which are conducted by a central bank that cause changes in its official reserves.

It is sale or purchase of its own currency in the exchange market in exchange for foreign currencies.

Foreign exchange reserves are the financial assets of the government held in the central bank. so, any addition to these reserves is shown on debit side.

Any withdrawal from the reserves is recorded on credit side.

Q. 3 Distinguish between balance of trade and BOP account.

Ans.:

BALANCE OF TRADE ACCOUNT	***BALANCE OF PAYMENTS ACCOUNT***
1. It is the difference between amount of exports and imports of goods.	1. It is an accounting statement showing systematic record of country sources and uses of foreign exchange during a given period of time.

(Contd...)

2. It is only a part of balance of payment a/c and is a narrow concept.	2. It includes balance of trade and is a wider concept.
3. It includes only visible items. It is a part of current account.	3. It includes both current and capital account.
4. Transactions of capital nature are not recorded.	4. Transactions of capital nature are recorded.

Q. 4 Differentiate between balance of trade and current account.

Ans.:

BALANCE OF TRADE	*CURRENT ACCOUNT*
1. It includes only visible items.	1. It includes both visible and invisible items.
2. It is a narrow concept since it is a part of current account	2. It is a wider concept since it includes balance of trade.

Q. 5 Distinguish between current and capital account.

Ans.:

CURRENT ACCOUNT	CAPITAL ACCOUNT
1. It records all the transactions relating to country's sources and uses of foreign exchange on account of flow of goods and services, unilateral transfers and incomes from and to abroad.	1. It records all the transactions relating to country's sources and uses of foreign exchange on account of transactions which cause changes in foreign financial assets and liabilities.
2. The components are: visibles and Invisibles (Services, unilateral transfers and income from and to abroad).	2. The components are: Investments to and from abroad, borrowings and lending, official reserve transactions.
3. It is a flow concept. *Examples:* Purchase and sale of machinery, services like shipping, banking etc.	3. It is a stock concept. *Examples:* Purchase of shares in foreign company, repayment of loan etc.

Q. 6 Differentiate between autonomous transactions and accommodating transactions.

Ans.:

AUTONOMOUS TRANSACTIONS	***ACCOMMODATING TRANSACTIONS***
1. International economic transactions which takes place due to some economic motive like earning profit.	1. Transactions that are undertaken to cover deficit or surplus on autonomous transactions.
2. These transactions are independents of all other balances of payment transactions. *Examples:* Export transactions to earn income, foreign investment to earn profit or interest are autonomous transactions.	2. These transactions are undertaken to correct the disequilibrium in autonomous transaction of balance of payment account. *Examples:* Borrowings from IMF (international monetary fund), external assistance from abroad to cover deficit are accommodating transactions.

Q. 7 Define deficit in balance of payment account.

Ans.: When total inflows on account of autonomous transactions are less than total outflow on account of such transactions, there is a deficit in the balance of payment account.

Suppose the autonomous inflow of foreign exchange during the year is \$ 600 while the total outflow is \$ 800 it means that there is a deficit of \$ 200.

BOARD QUESTIONS

Q. 1 Define 'Trade Surplus'. How is it different from 'Current Account surplus'? (CBSE 2019).

Q. 2 Explain the concept of 'deficit' in balance of payments. (CBSE 2018).

Q. 3 In which sub-account and on which, side of balance of payment account will foreign investments in India be recorded? Explain. (CBSE 2016).

Q. 4 Name the broad categories of transactions recorded in the 'capital account' of the Balance of payment accounts.

OR

Name the broad categories of transactions recorded in the current account of BOP. (CBSE 2015).

Q. 5 Where will sale of machinery to abroad be recorded in the BOP. Give reasons. (CBSE 2015).

Q. 6 Explain the meaning of balance of payments deficit. (CBSE 2014).

Q. 7 Differentiate between balance of trade and balance on current account. (CBSE 2013).

Q. 8 Distinguish between autonomous and accommodating transactions in BOP. Also explain meaning of 'deficit'. (CBSE 2012).

SAMPLE PAPERS

Sample Paper - I

Q:-1 Give the meaning of involuntary unemployment.

OR

Define exante saving. (1)

Q:-2 Deposits which are payable after the expiry of a fixed period are called **(1)**

(a) Time Deposits (b) Saving Deposits

(b) Both (a) & (b) (d) None of these

Q:-3 Capital loss can be defined as fall in the value of an asset due to **(1)**

(a) Forseen Obsolescence

(b) Unforseen Obsolescence

(c) Normal wear and tear

(d) Both (a) and (b)

Q:-4 Money supply is measured **(1)**

(a) At a particular point of time

(b) Over a period of time

(c) During the year only

(d) None of the above

Q:-5 What precautions should be taken while estimating national incomeby income Method **(3)**

OR

What precautions should be taken while estimating national income by expenditure method.

Q:-6 Calculate marginal propensity to consume from the following: **(3)**

(1) Equilibrium level of income ₹ 350

(2) Consumption expenditure at zero level of income ₹ 20

(3) Investment ₹ 50

Q:-7 What are the open market operations ? What is their effect on availability of credit? (4)

Q:-8 Explain the steps to be taken in deriving saving curve from the given consumption Curve. (4)

OR

Define multiplier. What is the relation of multiplier with marginal propensity to consume and marginal propensity to save.

Q:-9 Explain the concept of deficient demand. What is the role of reverse repo rate In removing this gap. (4)

Q:-10 Explain the following (6)

(1) Influencing allocation of resources

(2) Reducing inequalities of income

Q:-11(A) Explain the effect of depreciation of domestic currency on exports. (6)

State the two source each of demand and supply of foreign exchange.

Q:-12 From the following data, calculate the national income by income and output Method: (6)

Particulars	**(₹ in Crores)**
(i) Value of output of primary sector	1000
(ii) Value of output of secondary sector	400
(iii) Intermediate consumption of primary sector	500
(iv) Intermediate consumption of secondary sector	300
(v) Net factor income from abroad	- 5
(vi) Consumption of fixed capital	55
(vii) Indirect taxes	100
(viii) Subsidies	20
(ix) Mixed income of self employed	200
(x) Compensation of employees	170
(xi) Opening surplus	95

OR

Explain the circular flow of income with the help of a diagram.

Sample Paper - 2

Q:-1 Define induced investment **(1)**

Q:-2 What is the value of money multiplier and total deposit created if intial deposit is

₹ 200 crore and legal reserve ratio is 10 percent **(1)**

(a) 10, ₹ 1000 crore

(b) 10, ₹ 2000 crore

(c) 0.1, ₹ 1000 crore

(d) 0.1, ₹ 2000 crore

Q:-3 USA Embassy established in India is a part of economics territory of **(1)**

(a) India

(b) USA

(c) Both (a) & (b)

(d) None of the above

OR

Give two examples of flow concept.

Q:-4 Which of the following will increase the money supply ? **(1)**

(a) Increase in the reverse repo rate

(b) Increase in cash reserve ratio

(c) Purchase of securities in the open market

(d) Sale of the securities in the open market

Q:-5 Given nominal GDP, how can we find real GDP ? **(3)**

OR

Define operating surplus. State its components.

Q:-6 Calculate investment expenditure from the following data: **(3)**

(a) Equilibrium level of income	₹ 1000
(b) Marginal propensity to save	₹ 0.20
(c) Autonomous consumption expenditure	₹ 100

Q:-7 Distinguish between average propensity to save and average propensity to consume **(4)**

OR

Distinguish between marginal propensity to save and marginal propensity to consume.

Q:-8 What is an inflationary gap ? Explain the role of cash reserve ratio in removing this gap. **(4)**

Q:-9 Explain 'Banker to the government' as a function of Central bank. **(4)**

Q:-10 Differentiate between: **(6)**

(a) Revenue expenditure and capital expenditure

(b) Revenue receipts and capital receipts

OR

Define revenue deficit ? what are its implications. Give two measures to reduce this deficit.

Q:-11(A) Explain the meaning of 'deficit' in Balance of payment account. **(6)**

(B) Distinguish between autonomous and accommodating transactions of Balance of payment account.

Q:-12 (A) Calculate value added from the following **(3)**

(a) Industry A sells 200 units to B, 400 to C and imports 150 units

(b) Industry B sells 100 units to C, 500 to government and export 200 units.

(c) Industry C sells 700 units and 100 units used for self consumption.

(B) Calculate gross National product at market price using income method. (3)

		(₹)
(a)	Employers contribution to social security schemes	400
(b)	Depreciation	0.50
(c)	Dividends	100
(d)	Net factor income from abroad	200
(e)	Interest	300
(f)	Subsidies	800
(g)	Rent	200
(h)	Mixed Income of self employed	100
(i)	Profits	400
(j)	Wages and salaries	300
(k)	Operating surplus	1000
(l)	Net indirect taxes	100

Sample Paper - 3

Q:-1 Define reverse repo rate. **(1)**

OR

State the two approaches for determining the equilibrium level of income.

Q:-2 Legal reserve ratio includes **(1)**

(a) Cash reserve ratio and bank rate.

(b) Cash reserve ratio and reverse repo rate.

(c) Statutory liquidity ratio and cash reserve ratio

(d) Statutory liquidity ratio and bank rate.

Q:-3 National income estimated at constant price is known as: **(1)**

(a) Nominal national Income

(b) Real National Income

(c) Constant National Income

(d) Both (b) and (c)

Q:-4 Money supply includes **(1)**

(a) Currency held outside the banks and time deposits

(b) Currency held outside the banks and saving account deposits

(c) Currency held outside the banks and demand deposits

(d) None of the above

Q:-5 Define externalities . Give an example of negative externality. What is its Impact on welfare. **(3)**

OR

Explain the concept of mixed income of self employed with the help of an example.

Q:-6 As a result of increase in investment by ₹ 20 crore national income increases by ₹ 100 crore. Find out marginal propensity to consume. **(3)**

Q:-7 Differentiate between inflationary gap and deflationary gap **(4)**

OR

Explain the steps to be taken in deriving consumption curve from the saving curve.

Q:-8 If planned savings are greater than planned investment what will be Its effects On Inventories ? **(4)**

Q:-9 Explain Banker's bank and supervisor as a function of central bank. (4)

Q:-10 Define fiscal deficit. What are its implications. Give two measures to Reduce This deficit. (6)

Q:-11 (A) Explain why there is rise in demand for foreign exchange when its price falls? (6)

(B) Define the following:

(i) fixed exchange rate

(ii) flexible exchange rate

(iii) managed floating rate

OR

Distinguish between:

(a) Balance of trade and balance on current account

(b) Balance on current account and balance on capital account.

Q:-12 Find out the missing values of operating surplus and gross domestic capital Formation: (6)

		₹
(i)	Compensation of employees	1000
(ii)	Operating surplus	?
(iii)	Employer's contribution to social security schemes	120
(iv)	Net exports	-30
(v)	Net indirect taxes	40
(vi)	Mixed income of self employed	600
(vii)	Net factor income to abroad	20
(viii)	Depreciation	40
(ix)	Gross national product at factor cost	2120
(x)	Private final consumption expenditure	1440
(xi)	Government final consumption expenditure	490
(xii)	Gross domestic capital formation	?

Q. 11 Explain the effect of changes in RRR on money supply.

Ans.: It is the interest rate at which the commercial banks can deposit their funds with the central bank.

- During inflation, central bank raises it which induces the banks to transfer more funds to central bank due to attractive interest rates.
- This reduces the liquidity with the commercial bank and effect their credit creation capability.
- During deflation, Central Bank lowers it, which induces the banks not to transfer more funds to central bank. this increases their credit creation power.

Q. 12 What is effect of change in margin requirements on money supply in the economy?

Ans.: It is discount fixed by the central bank on the security mortgaged by the borrower to the commercial banks.

For Example: If a borrower mortgaged an asset worth ₹ 50 Lakh as security with the bank and margin fixed by central bank is 30 percent then commercial banks are allowed to give maximum amount of loan ₹ 35 lakh.

- Rise in margin requirements discourages the borrowing capacity of public which decreases the money supply in the economy.
- A fall in margin requirements encourages the people to borrow more which increases the money supply in the economy.

Q. 13 Explain the effect of 'moral suasion' on money supply in the economy?

Ans.: When central bank gives oral or written advice to the commercial banks for expanding or restrict credit it is called moral suasion.

During inflation, it suggests for credit contraction.

During deflation, it suggests for credit expansion.

4–6 Mark Questions

Q. 1 Explain the process of money creation by the commercial banks with the help of numerical example.

Ans.: When the primary cash deposit in the banking system leads to multiple expansion in the total deposits it is known as money multiplier. It is determined by LRR (Legal Reserve Ratio).

$$\textbf{Deposit Multiplier} = \frac{1}{LRR}$$

- All transactions in the economy are routed through the commercial banks. The deposits held by banks are used for giving loans so the money borrowed by the borrowers again comes back to the bank in form of deposits.
- It is assumed that not all customers will turn up at the same day to withdraw their deposits so commercial banks keep a portion of deposits as reserves and lend the rest.
- Thus, there is constant flow of new deposits into the bank.
- The process of creation of money is explained with the help of numerical example.

Money Multiplier Table

Rounds	*Deposit Received*	*Loans*	*Reserves (LRR 20%)*
Initial	10,000	8,000	2,000
I	8,000	6,400	1,600
II	6,400	5,120	1,280
–	–	–	–
n^{th} Round	–	–	–
Total:	₹50,000	₹40,000	₹10,000

- Initially public deposit is ₹ 10,000 and LRR – 20 percent .
- It means that banks keep only ₹ 2000 as reserves and lend the remaining amount of ₹ 8000 by opening the accounts in the names of the borrowers. This is the first-round creation and equals 80 percent of initial deposit.
- Since all the transactions are routed through the banks, the money spent by the borrowers come back into the banks into the deposit accounts of those who have received the payment. this increases demand deposit by ₹ 8000.
- Now out of new deposits of ₹ 8000 the bank will keep 20 percent as reserve (i.e ₹ 1600) and lend the remaining amount (i.e. ₹ 6400).
- Again, this money will come back to the bank and this again increases demand deposit by ₹ 6400.
- The same process continues and with each round the total deposits with the bank's increases.
- The process comes to an end when total cash reserves become equal to initial deposit. So as per example, with the initial deposits of ₹10000, the commercial banks have created money of ₹ 50000.

i.e. Total Deposit	=	Initial Deposit x Money Multiplier $\left(\frac{1}{LRR}\right)$.
	=	10000 x $\left(\frac{1}{20\%}\right)$
	=	10000 x 5
	=	₹ 50000.

BOARD QUESTIONS

Q. 1 **Define credit multiplier. What role does it play in determining the credit creation power of the banking system? Explain with example (CBSE 2019).**

Q. 2 **Explain banker to government function of central bank. (CBSE 2017, 2013).**

OR

Explain role of reverse repo rate in controlling money Supply. (CBSE 2017, 2014).

Q. 3 **Explain how open market operations are helpful in controlling credit creation. (CBSE 2016).**

Q. 4 **Government of India has recently launched 'Jan DhanYojna' aimed at every household to have atleast one bank account in the country. Explain how deposits made under the plan are going to affect national income of the country. (CBSE 2015).**

Ans.:

- Opening more bank accounts means more bank deposits.
- More deposits mean increase in the lending capacity.
- More lending by banks means more investment in the country.
- More investment means more national income.

Q. 5 **Explain 'lender of last resort' function. (CBSE 2018, 2014, 2013)**

Q. 6 **Explain the credit creation of role of commercial banks with the help of a numerical example. (CBSE 2013)**

Q. 7 **Currency is issued by the central bank, yet we say that commercial banks create money. Explain. How is this money creation likely to affect the national income? (CBSE 2015)**

Ans.: Commercial banks create deposits by lending money to the investors. The rise in investment in the economy leads to rise in national income through the multiplier effect.